#TheSpiritOfThePURPLECow

Leadership, Followship & Other Mind-Bending Stuff...

JAMES GALLOWAY

RIVER

PUBLISHING

River Publishing & Media Ltd
Barham Court
Teston
Maidstone
Kent
ME18 5BZ
United Kingdom

info@river-publishing.co.uk

Unless otherwise indicated, all Scripture quotations are taken from the Holy Bible New International Version. Copyright © 1973, 1978, 1984 by Biblica

MSG - The Message. Copyright © 1993, 1994, 1995, 1996, 2000, 2001, 2002 by Eugene H. Peterson

NCV - The Holy Bible, New Century Version®. Copyright © 2005 by Thomas Nelson, Inc.

ISBN 978-1-908393-20-3
Printed in the United Kingdom

Contents

Dedication   5

Acknowledgements   7

What Others Are Saying About This Book...   9

Preface   11

PART ONE: SOMETHING IS MISSING
1.1 Church Works...   15
1.2 Church Doesn't Work   19
1.3 Here Is My Vision   23
1.4 A Different Perspective   27
1.5 Where Are The Workers?   31
1.6 Striving To Train   35
1.7 Triggering Followship   39
1.8 I Am Joseph   45

PART TWO: FOLLOWSHIP EXISTS
2.1 Further Defining Followship   51
2.2 Different Types of Followship   57
2.3 Selecting Leaders of Followship   61
2.4 Caught and Taught   65
2.5 Paul and Intentionality   69
2.6 The Law of Innovation   73

2.7 #GoGetTheFANTASTICPeople 77

2.8 Leadership is Visual 81

PART THREE: ESTABLISHING FOLLOWSHIP

3.1 Creating Buzz 87

3.2 Social Media and BBM 91

3.3 Catalysts For Growth 95

3.4 Doing Life and Being Church 99

3.5 Creating a Whinge Free Environment 103

3.6 Team Driven 107

3.7 Rocks & Crocks 111

3.8 Three Chairs 117

PART FOUR: PRACTICAL WORKING EXAMPLES

4.1 The Art of Delegation 125

4.2 Understanding Natural, Zonal and Positional Leadership 129

4.3 Checks and Balances 133

4.4 Triangular Leadership 139

4.5 Perpetual Memory 145

4.6 Keys, Money & Mobile Phones 149

4.7 Stop Looking For Permission 155

4.8 Dying Church and "5" 159

4.9 Breaking the Rules and Invisible Ceilings 165

Epilogue | #TheSpiritOfThePURPLECOW 169

About the Author 173

Dedication

Dedicated to the leadership and followship that make Breathe City Church so irresistible...

Becky and I love you SO much and are SO privileged to have you with us on this absolutely awesome adventure.

Acknowledgements

To Jesus, who continues to allow me to be involved in this incredible adventure.

To Becky and our children: you are all my anchor.

To "Team BCC" who have stuck with me throughout the development of this book. You are truly a world class team.

To Jonathan and Pam Bugden, for your continued friendship, encouragement and wisdom.

To Tim Pettingale, for his expertise in understanding book writing.

To Steffy Hodgson, as she continues to assist and correct my work.

To Georgina Garratt and her ability to sort out my life.

To Jonathan Shearman for the breakfasts we had where we formed the concept of this book.

To Pastor Bill Hybels, his team, and the Willow Creek Community Church, who inspired and gave me permission to be me.

And to all BCCers everywhere for being the absolute example of the leadership/followship model!

What Others Are Saying About This Book...

"I first encountered James Galloway and Breath City Church in Stoke when I was invited to minister to their leaders. I was immediately impressed with this high calibre, committed and focussed group of people. It was a total joy to be with them. It is always a thrill to encounter those who see church as a dynamic adventure and who purposefully engage with its journey, as well as believing in its destiny. The world is not waiting for "another philosophy to believe in", but is hungry to encounter a community of people who behave what they believe, love the city and towns they are part of, and are willing to be agents of transformational change. Churches that see their buildings as "blessing boxes" in which to escape from the world have no future. Christians whose benchmark of success is taking the glory of God from where it is to where it isn't are the shapers of the future and those who God will use to usher in His Kingdom."
John Glass, General Superintendent of Elim Churches

"This book makes me smile - intentionally of course! I smile because James doesn't do or write anything unintentionally, and that same spirit – the spirit of the PURPLE COW – permeates the church he leads. Their purposeful, directed and totally intentional approach to building church in the 21st century is an inspiration to all who both lead and follow. This book about that process will make you think and challenge some preconceived notions about the way church should be done. But most of all it will make you intentional in what you do, which gets results. And then you will smile too!"
Stephen Matthew, Abundant Life Church

"James Galloway is creative, courageous and compassionate. *The Spirit of the Purple Cow* and what God is doing at and through Breathe City Church is compelling and challenging. Read it out of curiosity – the breadcrumbs you pick up have the potential of multiplying."
Canon J. John, Philo Trust

"In every part of society, from time to time, a unique 'maverick' appears who has something different, unique and important to say. If James can write a Christian leadership book under the title, *The Spirit of the Purple Cow*, he might just qualify for the above description! Wise people invest time in things that have the potential to both challenge, help and change them. That is why you should read this book."
David Shearman, Christian Centre, Nottingham

"For all of us who love the building of God's Church, this is an inspiring book. Better still, it's written by a man at the centre of his calling, who has the passion, mandate and growing experience to see God's people do God's work. Anyone who believes (as James does) that Stoke is 'the centre of the universe' has to be a man of great faith! But having seen he, Becky, and their team build something unique in the Potteries, I believe they've experienced something the rest of us need to see and understand. I ask you to take James and his team very seriously indeed, for God is using them all in some truly spectacular ways."
Fergus Scarfe, God TV

"What can I say about James Galloway – one of the most inspiring motivational leaders; true, gritty; he is the real deal bringing a new, relevant style of leadership to UK churches. I can highly recommend this book – you need to read this!"
Ben Cooley, CEO Hope for Justice

Preface

I have to be honest from the very outset. It is absolutely absurd that a 37-year old bloke from Stoke is writing this book. Furthermore, I have only been a senior pastor for four years and I am learning every step of the way.

I was cheeky enough to respond to the request to write *From Beach Hut to Palace – a story of church repurposed*, my first book. That story is our story and has grown and moved on since then. The book proved a great success. I wrote a successful book; I am a published author!

Yes, it was cheeky to write that book, so why on earth am I writing this book? This one can only be put down to sheer audacity!

What on earth do I know? Well, I don't think the answer I want to give is *what I know*. This is more about *how I know*.

I can say with absolute confidence that Jesus is building His Church! We are privileged to play our part in fleshing out His Plan A. We host many a leader who asks about our considerable growth in such a short space of time, about the quality of leaders who have gathered around Becky and I, and about the rapid growth of maturity in the people. How did all this happen? I say to them what I say to you, reader, now: "On most days, I have no idea!"
It's not *what* I know that I unpack in this conversation, it's *how* I know. This book is a paradigm shift.

At this point, I presume you'd like to know about the meaning of the title: *The Spirit of the Purple Cow*. I could explain now, but

I address this at the end of the book and first we have to go on a journey.

I reiterate: this book is a paradigm shift. I'm sure it may teach you nothing new, but my prayer is that it will help you apply your knowledge in a more effective manner in the 21st Century.

What do I mean by this exactly? Well, there has been a huge shift in the culture and mindset of the 20th and 21st centuries and this has had an immense outworking throughout life, society and the Church.

Television is a good example of the shift that has taken place. 20th Century television said, "As long as I produce better stuff than the other two or three programmes that are on at the same time, then I will progress."

21st Century television says, "It's not a competitive market any more. There are too many channels and programmes available. Therefore, it's about being the best we can be, being accessible – and those who resonate with what we are producing will watch."

Two different paradigms that produce different results.

So, understanding that a cultural shift has taken place, this book unpacks a fresh look at church. It allows the reader to move from an historical view, a present view, even a future view, to viewing church with a *forward thinking memory*. This book seeks to train the reader to think very differently regarding the building of church. It trains the reader to view things from the future backwards – to develop the art of being INTENTIONAL.

Part One:
Something is Missing

1.1 | Church Works

Words.

They are everywhere. Spoken so frequently that most of the words uttered are missed. Words are spoken and then mostly vanish into thin air. My father always said, "When everything is said and done, there is usually more said than done."

We waste words.

God doesn't.

In fact, Scripture tells us that His words are never wasted. They fail *"to return void"* (Isaiah 55:11). Scripture reveals something of the personality of God when it reveals His first recorded words:

"...then God said, 'Let there be light,' and there was light."

It's an inherent part of God's personality that His words bring both revelation and delivery on His promises.

John tells us that the "Word" became flesh and made His home amongst us. Incarnational word – a delivered promise; a fulfilled word.

This Word is Jesus.

If Jesus is God's Word incarnate, then when He promises to do something, we can be assured that it will be delivered. When

Jesus says that something is going to happen, it's a sure thing. His promises are something we can base our lives on, be totally reliant upon.

When Jesus says, *"I will build my Church,"* what we have is God's Word made flesh promising something. Just as light is still travelling at the speed of light because God said, *"Let there be...",* so His promise to build His Church is also utterly guaranteed.

Jesus *is* building His Church.

The thing that surprises me most about this is the fact that, as far as I can see, the Church is the one, single thing that Jesus has said He is committed to building. We have the absolute assurance that God's Word made flesh promises to build one thing: His Church.

So at the very outset of this book, let's make a few things clear.

First, I am absolutely convinced that God is real! Therefore, there is no doubt in my heart or mind that what He says is true. His words have been proven true, time and time again. I know Him to be a deliverer on His promises. Jesus is!

My perceptions of God and His promises could be tainted by the fact that when I or others make promises, sometimes they aren't delivered on. Okay, let's be real ... most of the promises we make aren't delivered on. It's not that we recklessly make promises, it's simply that we very often don't have the power, authority or capacity to fulfil the promises we've made. Broken promises, therefore, fill us with a hint of hopelessness when further promises are made. We want a "receipt" for those promises in case we have to bring them back. We don't want to hand over the cash, or the currency of "trust", until we receive delivery.

However, with God it isn't like that. He has a track record of delivery. It was His Son, whom God promised, who then made the promise to build His Church. Let's lay this to rest at the very outset: *eradicate any thought or preconceived notion that not all promises are delivered on.*

Second, I understand that there are many promises in Scripture which are conditional. They are the "If you ... then I will" type of promises of God. This isn't one of them. In Matthew 16:18 there is no condition attached to Jesus' promise. It is as simple a promise as you'll find anywhere in Scripture. God's Word made flesh clearly maps out for the whole of eternity to note: I WILL BUILD MY CHURCH.

Third, let's make something else very clear. Jesus has assumed full responsibility for the building of His Church.

There are some things that we are responsible for ourselves. We are told, for instance, to *"Work out our salvation with fear and trembling"* (Philippians 2:12). The Bible makes it very clear that the responsibility for this is ours. It is our salvation, our working it out, our fear and trembling – no one else's. The Bible doesn't play games with us. The responsibility is ours.

But when Jesus, God's Word made flesh, says, I WILL BUILD MY CHURCH, please take note of the ownership and responsibility to deliver on this promise. As we are responsible for our salvation, He is responsible for building His Church.

This highlights Jesus' incredible passion and commitment to deliver on His promise. He publicly takes all the responsibility to deliver onto His own shoulders for this one thing He says He is going to build. He doesn't pass the buck or infer that it is anyone else's responsibility. It's His.

Please note the severity of Jesus' statement.

When Jesus was praying on the Mount of Olives, He prayed a prayer that revealed SO much. He prayed,

"Father, if you are willing, please take this cup of suffering from me."

Then He re-aligned His prayer with the purposes of God the Father:

"...yet I want your will to be done."

We know that Jesus had already said, *"I only do what I see the Father do"* and, *"I have only come to do the will of the Father"* (John 5:19, 6:38). So when Jesus says...

"You are blessed, Simon son of John, because my Father in heaven has revealed this to you. You did not learn this from any human being. Now I say to you that you are Peter and on this rock I will build my church, and the powers of hell will not conquer it." (Matthew 16:17-18)

...we know that His words reflect the will of the Father. Jesus got permission from His Father to be adamant about the fact that He is now going to build the Church.

I think I've made my point strongly enough.

It is my firm opinion that church works.

It is a sure thing that Jesus is building His Church – and if He says it, then it is pretty ridiculous to believe that it won't work or that He will fail and not deliver. If there is anything we can be sure of, it is that Jesus is building His Church. Just as we are confident that light exists and is still travelling at the speed of light, we can be confident that Jesus is building His Church and will continue to do so.

1.2 | Church Doesn't Work

Andrew Hackney, Paul Challinor and I were the privileged young boys who got to be in charge of the Overhead Projector in our church services in the 1980s. Every Sunday the OHP rota would be released and I would passionately look to see whether my name was on the list. This list and the one that told me whether I had made the school football team were the two things I cared about most – that's how passionate I was about church.

You may laugh, but I had perfected the art of the OHP, even down to the speed at which I could follow the worship leader as they switched songs (or choruses as we called them in those days) midway through, 1980s style. The boxes of OHPs were always in alphabetical order (I made sure they were beforehand) and I had memorised the first lines of all the verses and choruses in my diligence to serve.

In the 90s, however, my services on the OHP were no longer needed as we got all "21st Century". As we geared up for the new millennium OHPs were being replaced with projectors. These new gadgets were all the rage and so multimedia was thrust into the Church. Immediately, I embraced this novel way of helping the congregation engage.

Just as technology moved on and we figured out how to adapt and apply it to our situation, conversations about the best way to "do church" changed and different theories emerged. In the 00s the conversation moved on again and, for the first time, the concept of "repurposing church" emerged. "Emergent church", "Fresh Expressions" and the like were phrases used to describe this new thinking. Heck, my first book, *From Beach Hut to Palace* was a story of "church repurposed".

So here we are now, in the second decade of the 21st Century and *change* or *changing* is still at the forefront of the Church and its conversation. Statistics show us that all the methods and novel ideas that we have had are not working. People are leaving the Church in their thousands. Recently, on a family holiday in North Wales I was horrified at the number of church buildings I saw that had been left empty and derelict or were being used for other means. In my home city of Stoke-on-Trent, church buildings are, embarrassingly, a popular topic of the local press, as they are becoming dangerous eyesores that Lottery funding must now address. Denominations are announcing record losses and predicting their imminent closure unless something changes. The average age of church attendees is frightening when examined, indicating that if we fail to attract new, younger people, then natural progression will mean that churches will die out very rapidly in the next 20 years.

There seems to be a huge push to engage with the Google Generation, but overall this also seems to be showing little fruit. Pockets of great stories and rallying calls go out for the cause, but resistance is futile... It seems we have a cancerous epidemic of dying church. "Houston, we have a problem..." is a famous quote that seems appropriate to the Church right now.

In short, the Church isn't working. Or is it?

I am not much of an academic or scholar of Church history, or a theologian for that matter. I do, however, have eyes in my head. Observation teaches us many things if we dare to open our eyes.

I was always taught to look for the continuum, the common thread.

I can clearly see two threads. First, there is Jesus who made His commitment, promise and public confession that He would build

His Church. Second, there is "us" and our clear and documented passion for bringing change to make this thing called church work.

Let's take the first thread: Jesus. Has He got it wrong? Is He failing to deliver on His promise? Does He not have the capacity or power to fulfil His word? Well, evidently the painful picture I painted above is not the total or full picture. Jesus is most definitely building His Church! Across the planet sensational stories are told of Jesus building His Church. More people are coming to Christ now than ever in history. Explosive growth of His Church is being experienced daily on many continents of the globe. Right now in my nation of the UK, many churches are seeing explosive growth and it is more than simply transition-growth. New birth is happening in a powerful way. The church where I'm privileged to be lead pastor, Breathe City Church, is continuing to grow at an unprecedented rate. In four years we have seen it grow from 62 people to now fast approaching 1,000 people gathering every Sunday and 70% of our growth has been new birth. Our story is one of many stories.

Jesus is building His Church!

Now look at the second thread: us. If the Church has a problem, it lies not with Jesus; it lies with us. How come there is such a contrast of stories above?

Stories of panic and an epidemic of failing churches and destitute, decaying buildings, contrast with stories of thriving congregations seeing huge numbers of people gather every week.

This book is designed to examine and unpack this frustration: *Church works. Church doesn't work.* What is the difference? How come in some places it's happening and in others it's not? Is Jesus selective? Are some people more holy or hungry than others? Does Jesus have favourites? Is it a style thing? What's the deal?

There must be a difference. But it can't be style or flavour or levels of holiness or standards of excellence, because the spectrum and diversity of churches experiencing growth is so broad. There are thriving traditional churches as well as our experience here at

Breathe City Church as a young, modern church. Both are equally valid and experiencing great moves of God. There is explosive growth in churches found in large urban populations, but churches in rural areas are experiencing the same. Jesus is building His Church, but at the same time we have the frustration that church doesn't work.

You may be a leader or a member of a local congregation or even a person who is totally disengaged with church. I hope this book helps you.

I hope and pray that by the end of this journey we will have some revelation and experience release, so that we can all experience what it is to see Jesus building His Church.

1.3 | Here Is My Vision

Let's begin this exploration by unpacking the "standard" way of building church. As an aside, let's be mature enough to recognise that we all know it is *Jesus* who is building His Church. What we are discussing here are systems and leadership tools that are required for the Church to be built. We all recognise that Jesus builds His Church and he uses people to do it.

Great.

Now that's out of the way let's move on.

The standard way of building church begins with a person – a leader or a group of people with a person at the helm having a heart, desire, passion, conviction, a word from God, an invitation or a mandate to establish an expression of church which is linked to a geography, demographic, a style of church or a type of community.

The general protocol is to start with establishing a Purpose Statement or reason for being. This may take a variety of forms but, since Jesus is building His Church, the purpose is associated with Him. Purpose statements will therefore naturally tend to focus on glorifying God, reaching the lost, creating an environment in which people can hear Jesus' message and be discipled, and so on.

These central aims will be expressed in a variety of different ways, but essentially they are the reason we do church.

Having established a purpose, next comes the development of a "Vision". The Vision is the vehicle that facilitates the purpose. It is what the purpose looks like when mobilised. The Vision tends to be birthed by those in the church considered to be "visionaries" and will come out of their experience, background, perception and/or focus. This is the wonder of the Church: in our diversity we are able to see a spectrum of activity that we should celebrate and not criticise.

The Church of Jesus Christ, with all its diversity, is something to behold!

Following on from Purpose and Vision, our Culture or Values are established. Culture dictates the way in which we do things, our behaviour and priorities, what is important to us and how we conduct ourselves. My last book, on this subject, really did help many churches and leaders and we will be addressing this subject later.

Fourthly, there is a focus upon Structure or Operation. This has to do with the mechanics of the activities of the church, how it works and the systems that cause a smooth movement. For any organisation that is primarily dependant upon volunteers this is critical and delicate. We will also look at this in detail later in the book.

All of the above usually takes place at a leadership or team level. Once these elements are ready and in place, then the overall concept needs to be communicated to the church. This will often happen through a "Vision Sunday" or simply a "here are our plans" type of event. What we hope the future will look like is rolled out to the congregation and they embrace it with joy (or not, depending on the health of the church), God blesses it and that, as they say, is history.

This may all sound very twee, but in reality, many a church leader, including myself, has stood in front of a congregation and done exactly this: communicated a message regarding what the future holds, having no real idea of whether it will become a reality or not. Yes, this is done in faith and with a right heart, but as we have already noted: Church works and (in the same breath) Church doesn't work. Often, for a variety of reasons, the vision seems to drift into oblivion and the congregation never sees it fulfilled. What is the issue? Is the purpose, vision, values, culture or structure to blame? Did we get it wrong or were we just naive?

In Luke 8 we see Jesus tell a story that is very often used in Kids Church. It will be very familiar to you, but maybe not in this context.

"'A farmer went out to plant his seed. As he scattered it across his field, some seed fell on a footpath, where it was stepped on, and the birds ate it. Other seed fell among rocks. It began to grow, but the plant soon wilted and died for lack of moisture. Other seed fell among thorns that grew up with it and choked out the tender plants. Still other seed fell on fertile soil. This seed grew and produced a crop that was a hundred times as much as had been planted!" When he had said this, he called out, 'Anyone with ears to hear should listen and understand.'"

In Jesus' parable, the farmer scattered seed on four types of ground: the footpath, the rocks, the thorns and the fertile ground. Only the seed that fell on the fertile ground produced a substantial harvest. Many a church leader or pastor stands in front of his or her congregation and begins to scatter their seed, hoping and desiring that it will produce a harvest. They diligently scatter the vision, hoping and praying it takes root and begins to strongly grow, producing evidenced fruit and a harvest of people and lives affected by the power of the Gospel.

Some of his or her words fall on the footpath where it gets stepped on and the birds of the air take it away. Other words fall on hard, rocky ears and hearts that initially grow but soon wither and die due to lack of moisture or fluidity. Further words fall amongst the thorns that strangle the life out of anything that has life which can be strangled out of it.

Finally, however, some words fall on good soil. In every church there is good soil. This is the fertile ground. This is where the difference lies. This is where vision can become a reality and hopes can be fulfilled. This is where the difference lies between what we see thriving in church life and what we see failing in church life.

It is my suggestion that 75% of vision is never fulfilled in this scenario. This percentage is the reason there is such a gulf between the great stories of church life and the horror stories. This percentage is what is evident across numerous churches today. By this I am not being dismissive of 75% of the people in our churches or of church itself. But understanding that this divide exists will, if we recognise it, change our strategy of seeing church built.

Let's continue our journey of discovery.

1.4 | A Different Perspective

We serve a perfect God. Jesus, who is building His Church is perfect. His Church, which He is building, is not! I know when we meet Him we will be made like Him (1 John 3:2), but right now ... the Church is not perfect!

The famous anonymous quote says that, "If you find the perfect church, don't join it because you'll spoil it." Never a truer word has been uttered.

But the fact is, though we love people and have their best interests at heart, have a passion for the Church and a commitment to our communities, genuinely believe that Jesus is building His Church AND that we are standing in faith to see that vision fulfilled, we forget one thing ... not all ground is fertile and not all seed will be received!

Genesis 1 tells us that God instructed Adam to be fruitful and multiply, to fill the earth and govern it. As the Church we see this as our responsibility and want to be salt and light and make a difference. But we forget something. This instruction was given to Adam who had not yet sinned. To the fallen Adam, then, God in His grace gave him some inside information to help him with this mandate.

Genesis 3:23 says,

*"God sent Adam out to **cultivate** the ground from which he had been made."*

The Church is not perfect. Neither are you. Neither am I. But Jesus loves us and we're in His grace. Jesus, the Word made flesh, is full of grace AND truth (John 1:14). Like Adam, we need to learn that "to cultivate" is a vital part of our activity.

The ground upon which vision is cast, whether that be in church life or your own personal walk, can be a pathway, rocks, thorns or fertile soil … but it doesn't have to be. The farmer could have been really smart and scattered the seed only on fertile ground, ignoring the thorns, rocks and pathway, thus producing a 100% return on his efforts and not wasting 75% of his seed.

BINGO!

100%!

But you and I both know that this is not how Jesus works and thus it is not how Jesus builds His Church. John's Gospel reminds us that Jesus uses a very powerful word that we often forget:

WHOSOEVER! (see John 3:15, John 4:14 and John 11:26)

Luke 19:10 informs us that Jesus came to seek and to save those who are lost and far off.

Jesus most definitely wants His seed, His message, His word to fall on fertile ground. But then what about the pathway, the thorns and the rocks?

Cultivate!

Luke 3:23 tells us that,

"Jesus was known as the son of Joseph…"

I think that you and I agree that this identity didn't sculpt His destiny. Instead, knowing that He was the Son of God defined His behaviour and guided the outcome of His life.

Many a person has had their destiny defined by their natural environment. Many a church has had its outcome determined by "the way things have always been". But we are called to be defined by the God-definition of who we are.

Cultivate!

The year I fell in love with Becky was pretty spectacular! It was probably the first year that I had a shower and used aftershave. Most guys pretty much stink until they meet The One and then they clean themselves up and pursue them with all that they have in their heart (and pocket). The day Becky said she would marry me was SUCH a highlight. The day we were married was awesome. 11 years later I realised that I'd become fat and lazy!

I'd changed from the eager, excited young man in love that I was ... into a slob! (I've now rectified the scenario you'll be pleased to know).

What happened? When I had a clear focus and goal I stepped up. But when I had achieved that goal I regressed to my default position.

All of us have a default position. If we are to live according to the God-definition of who we are, we have to change. We have to change our default settings!

Cultivate!

If church is to become all that Jesus intends, we have to change our default settings.

Cultivate!

If the farmer is to scatter his seed on more than merely the fertile ground he has to decide to not be lazy and simply hope, but begin intentionally cultivating the pathway, the rocky ground and the thorny ground. Once the ground is cultivated he can then scatter his seed and see a 100% harvest. Merely scattering vision, praying and hoping that it catches on fertile ground is admirable, but why waste 75% of the potential?

We have to develop a different perspective on things. We have to develop an *intentional framework* of thought and operation in order to see the harvest that we have the potential for. The seed that is in the farmer's hand carries the potential and DNA for life, for a harvest. It is the farmer's responsibility, realising that there is no such thing as a perfect environment, to intentionally set to work, cultivating the ground where he is called; to be fruitful and multiply; to rule and reign over it.

Remember, Jesus' passionate statement in Matthew 16 had no conditions or excuses attached. He is committed to building His Church. He also states that *"the fields are white to harvest"* (Matthew 9:37), so He also knows the condition of the ground in which the seed is to be sown.

But He's still making no excuses – and neither should the Church!

Jesus is building His Church. His promise is being fulfilled and His seed is producing a harvest where the ground is being cultivated.

Let's move on and explain a little more...

1.5 | Where Are The Workers?

As we continue to unpack this embryonic thought, let's move to a different angle of approach.

What know that Jesus is building His Church. He has committed Himself to this and the power of His Word (seed) has the potential for 100% harvest. However, the present paradigm we possess is that we present vision and then build church in an environment where potentially will see at least 75% of everything we're believing for wasted before we have even started.

In order to address this, we have to grasp hold of an *intentional mindset* and engage in activity that will cultivate the ground before the seed is scattered.

1 Samuel 14 contains one of my favourite passages of Scripture.

It tells of Jonathan who is frustrated by the lack of progress the Israelite army is making against the Philistine army. He is so infuriated with this situation that he breaks rank. He turns to his armour bearer and says, *"Come on, let's go over to where the Philistines have their outpost ... Perhaps the Lord will help us"* (1 Samuel 14:1,6).

There are three things that occur next that I wish to highlight and draw to our attention.

First, there is the response of the armour bearer. He defiantly and bravely, without hesitation, responds, "Do whatever you think is best ... I'm completely with you, whatever you decide." Total, unshakable loyalty.

Second, there is the reaction of Saul in verses 16-19. We're told that the commotion caused by Jonathan and his armour bearer was "a strange sight" and Saul called for a roll call to occur in order to discover who was missing. Then he called for the ephod. Saul tried to interpret what was happening with strategies that had previously worked, were tried and tested. Yet we are told that Saul eventually says,

"Never mind, let's get going!" (v19)

Third, there is the change in activity of the 600 soldiers and those hiding (see verse 2 and 20-23). The 600 soldiers were chilling under the pomegranate tree. The king's son shouldn't have gone on this deadly adventure, they should have. However, when Jonathan and his armour bearer broke through, the soldiers joined in the roar and they experienced victory together. Note also the Hebrews who were hiding in the caves: when they began to get a sniff of victory they came out from their hiding places. There was no mention of cowardice and again they shared in the victory.

In summary, the previous generation didn't necessarily understand what was going on, but they saw that they had to get involved; those who were in comfort roused themselves and got involved; those who were hiding and fearful escaped the prison of the caves and got involved.

Jonathan saw his vision of the Lord, acted on their behalf and ALL experienced victory.

However the key, the linchpin, the juxtaposition in this whole story, and the revelation for me is this:

"I'm completely with you, whatever you decide!"

I genuinely think Jonathan would have not initiated this victory if it was not for the response of his armour bearer.

The armour bearer is the key to the king's victory. He demonstrated what I like to call "followship".

The followship that occurred in this story shows that the greatest vision can be cast, but what is essential is a great commitment to executing it. Without followship, victory would have not been achieved.

The example of this armour bearer and the results that are in Scripture for us to see are so powerful. I believe that the Church needs to grasp this revelation. Vision is not key. Strategy is not key. Culture is important. Purpose is important also. A "Jonathan" is obviously part of the activity, otherwise we cannot get to the "Perhaps the Lord will help us..." The genius key then, is finding the armour bearers.

What do Armour Bearers look like?

Jesus tells us that the harvest is plentiful but that the "workers" are few (Matthew 9:37). Jonathan had just one armour bearer, so yes, the workers were few – but look at the profound effect that was achieved by just one person skilled in the art of followship.

Armour Bearers are people of influence. One man's actions resulted in a change of activity of 600 soldiers and those hiding in caves. Jonathan didn't have to lobby the 600 or those hiding – he just asked for the involvement of the one who would stimulate the involvement of the many.

Yes, the workers are few, but enthusiasm is contagious.

Armour Bearers are people of commitment. "Do whatever you think is best" demonstrates that the armour bearer was not in this for himself or for a reward. "Whatever" implies that his focus was Jonathan. Armour Bearers are made of substance not show. They have depth, significance, virtue and close proximity. Jonathan didn't have to shout. The armour bearer was close by.

Armour Bearers are people of adventure. When "whatever you decide" is uttered it shows a spirit of adventure. He could have at least asked about the plans before committing, but no, he was a person of adventure. 600 were in comfort and many others were in hiding, but the armour bearer was hungry for adventure.

Armour Bearers are people of Now. If you look at Jonathan's language in verse 1 it is easy to discover the time schedule of activity. Scripture introduces the story with "one day". This adventure could have taken place on any day, at any time. We don't know whether this armour bearer's training was complete or whether he was training "on the job", but the point is, he responded to Jonathan's "Come on, let's go!" So similar to Jesus calling His first disciples in the gospel of John (1:43) with the words, *"Come, follow me."*

Armour Bearers are the people who go with the leader and carry the weight. Their role is to cultivate and prepare by going where others will follow. They are always the first on the scene; they are "respond first" type people. To be hesitant is not in their genetic makeup. Evidently, it didn't take much for Jonathan's words to settle in the fertile heart of the armour bearer. Armour bearers are the fertile soil.

1.6 | Striving To Train

Due to the unreserved acknowledgement that "the workers are few", there has been a monumental increase in the volume of training made available in the present day, which I wholeheartedly endorse.

But with regard to the armour bearer, we have to understand that ministry development and opportunity in church life is not what this type of person is after. As leaders, we want to develop those people who will intentionally cultivate areas of church life in order that the "seed" or vision that we sow will be fulfilled and yield a harvest. Armour bearers are the people naturally suited to this task.

Again, the story of Jonathan and his armour bearer in 1 Samuel 14 provides our context. Armour bearers are actually leaders who have a number of traits which we can see as follows:

The first and most obvious trait is that **they don't fit the mould**. I will come back to this in a few page's time, but we have to highlight the fact that Jonathan hadn't told his father what he was doing and the armour bearer didn't have a problem with this. Armour bearers don't follow regular, standard or expected patterns. My close friend Clive Urquhart, who is doing a sensational job of leading the incredible church Kingdom Faith, once highlighted the fact that some people are not meant to fit, they are meant to shape. Armour bearers don't fit the mould; they are unique. In my situation, I instantly think of my Executive Pastor, Paul Jukes. He is unique, doesn't fit the mould and is absolutely my armour bearer.

The second trait is that **they are happy to remain anonymous**. In other words, there is no edge to them, no ego. They are not trying to make a name for themselves and they are absolutely assured in their gifting to be an armour bearer to a Jonathan. Many Jonathans, however, because of the gift and skill set that their armour bearers carry, do become insecure, even jealous. This is the downside of many a leader. If we are to continue this journey we have to address this issue. The visionary leader doesn't have to be the best at everything. They are called and anointed to be the visionary leader – they simply see, communicate and lead. Armour Bearers need to be able to function in their God-given calling. They aren't seeking the stage or a platform, but they'll evidently get it due to "the gift making way for the giver".

Jonathan, don't exasperate your armour bearer!

The third and most wonderful trait is that **they are people of integrity**. Jonathan's armour bearer was interested in him doing what he thought best (1 Samuel 14:7). The integrity of an armour bearer ensures that a Jonathan stays on track with the course that God has set. With the harvest so plentiful and the workers so few it would be easy to simply pursue the fertile field next door, rather than continually and intentionally cultivating the field and mission that God has assigned the leader to. In our own experience at BCC, because of what has happened with our growth and profile, very often we are invited to plant churches in other cities – cities to which we are not called. Armour bearers help to keep me on track and not get carried away. Remember the initial instruction of God to Adam: to be fruitful and multiply, to reign and rule. This doesn't necessarily mean to be popular and have many supporters. It means to be diligent in effecting change and seeing the dominion of the King (King-dom) established in the field where he has assigned us.

A final trait of the armour bearer is that **they are loyal**. At no point in 1 Samuel 14 do we get the impression that the armour bearer fled. He isn't mentioned again after this passage, but Scripture never states that he leaves Jonathan's side. Loyalty in this present generation is a sight to be seen and applauded. Those who possess this trait haven't learned it – it is a God-given ability to go beyond the call of duty.

With these traits in mind, training the workers becomes less of an academic process. I always endorse a more hands on approach; on the job activity.

As mentioned at the beginning, the armour bearer either had prior experience or he was learning as the adventure unfolded. Either way, Jonathan was not fussed. Too often we have concerns that people will not make the grade. But Jonathan was a visionary leader committed to fulfilling the mission. His focus was upon this and the armour bearer's focus was upon Jonathan. The key here is that leaders again need to take their attention off pastoring and start leading. Pastoring or mentoring will happen naturally with people who have fertile hearts. It's impossible to impose discipleship. Too often we try to disciple people who are not prepared to be discipled. A person can only be discipled if they choose to be.

Armour bearers have to be close to Jonathans. They have to hang out together, know each other. It is a relational process, not an institutional process. What the Jonathan needs to realise is that the armour bearer doesn't need molly-coddling – they are their own man (and woman) and they can take care of themselves. Actually, they are there to take care of Jonathan – so let them.

They are closer to the action. Thus Jonathan, although casting vision, needs to ensure that the armour bearer is being listened to.

What is happening here? The process of creating a few armour bearers who understand "followship" is occurring. They in turn become leaders and so more followers emerge, who follow in the example of the armour bearers.

For too long leaders have been longing for people to follow, to grasp hold of their vision and run with it.

The reality is, it is possible to be very intentional and create the type of followers who will see the vision fulfilled.

1.7 | Triggering Followship

The question arises then, how do we trigger "followship"?

It simply doesn't just happen right?

Right!

It doesn't just happen!

The first thing to note is that followship has to be given something or someone to follow – leadership.

The second thing is that followship has to be given a mandate or a pathway or a journey. Followship, in its most innocent form is created when it follows a leader who is going somewhere, fulfilling something or moving somehow.

One of the most revealing activities that can be implemented to cause followship to occur is to develop an evangelistic strategy. You may be horrified to read this, but it is my view that most churches are generally not engaged in or set up for reaching the lost and those far away from God, because they have not thought strategically about evangelism.

The reason that an evangelistic strategy triggers followship is firstly because **it creates leadership**. The leader standing up and declaring "we are going for this" naturally creates an example to be followed. It is imperative that the leader themselves is enacting the strategy, and not just talking about it, so that the followers have someone to follow. If the senior pastor is not actively reaching the lost and those far away from God, then the people won't either. This is a terrible indictment of the Church in the UK, but I fundamentally believe that the reason why the UK is seeing so little new birth is because senior pastors have lost the understanding that they have to be the primary champion for reaching the lost. They have to be modelling it for others.

Please hear me, I recognise that all leaders are not evangelists. I am not an evangelist, but we must be doing the work of an evangelist. According to Jesus, He came to seek and save those who are lost and far from God (Luke 19:10). As the body of Christ, surely we should be following our Head's example.

One of the greatest shocks in my short tenure as a senior pastor was the day my neighbours came to church for the first time. It was great to see them and yet that wasn't the shock, that was a delight! The greatest shock came when, after the service, a new BCCer came to me and said, "That's why BCC is growing so fast! You're the first pastor I've had that has ever been able to say that your neighbours were in church."

Since then I have made it a habit to invite my neighbours and friends to come to BCC activities. It's a regular occurrence. Their spiritual journey is between them and God, but the front door of our church is wide, warm and receiving. It is that way because I, the leader, want it that way and model it that way. Bringing my world to the House of God is a normal activity. It's not strange or spooky or an occasional one-off. It is the way it should be.

Followship sees the model and follows!

Secondly, **an evangelistic model gives followship something tangible to work with**.

Our evangelistic model is really, really simple and heavily influenced by my time with Bill Hybels and his team at the sensational Willow Creek Community Church. This church has such a passion for those who are far away from God. My time there has had a dramatic impact on my leadership.

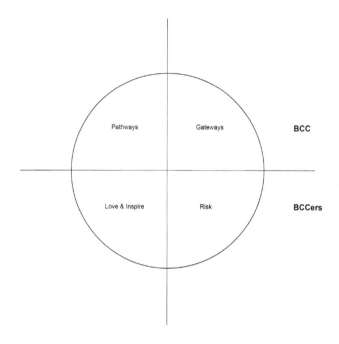

The strategy is expressed in two parts. The first is the responsibilities of BCC. The second is the responsibilities of BCCers.

BCC has a commitment to PATHWAYS. This means we ensure that we are always equipping and empowering BCCers to be sold out, effective, fully devoted followers of Christ. As leaders and pastors we are committed to bringing everything we have to the table to ensure they get exactly what is required to make an impact in their homes and communities and develop a Christ-centred approach to life. This includes working into our budgets the ability to bring the best ministries on the planet to BCC and never taking a mediocre approach to what we preach or teach. BCCers will have available to them a diverse range of PATHWAYS that they can jump on and see significant discipleship and advancement in their walk with Jesus. Whether that be leadership pathways, training pathways, ministry pathways or otherwise, we commit to creating the PATHWAYs for them to walk on.

BCC's second commitment is to make sure there are multiple and excellent GATEWAYS. We understand that relationships are not "microwavable"; that BCCers have been working on those relationships for years and years and years. Solid relationships aren't created in a microwave, they develop over time via a slow cooker. We don't want those relationships to suffer or be totally demolished in an instant because the GATEWAY is mediocre. We don't want BCCers friends saying, "I will never go to church with you again because it's rubbish!" or "Man, you guys are weird!" We want our GATEWAYS to be world class so that BCCers are so chuffed to be bringing their world into church. They must be confident that they won't be embarrassed or have to cringe. Many a Christian doesn't invite their friend to church because that relationship, which has been maturing in a slow cooker, is too precious to sacrifice if the GATEWAY is really dire.

So GATEWAYS must be excellent and multiple. A Sunday morning GATEWAY isn't enough. People have busy lives and the junior football league far outweighs church on a Sunday morning.

So how are our neighbours going to come? We have to be creative and provide multiple GATEWAYS.

BCCers have a commitment to two really simple parts of the strategy. The first is to love people for who they are and inspire people to be all that they can be.

Simple.

Be salt and light.

Love on people in your home and community.

Inspire people wherever you work, study or drink coffee.

Simple.

The second commitment BCCers have is to take the RISK! Many a Christian never invites a friend to church because they would rather not take the RISK.

BCC commits to working really hard at our GATEWAYS to provide BCCers with the best (mediocrity doesn't live here – our events and programmes are going to be world class) and in turn, the strategy for BCCers is to commit and take the RISK. Yes, relationships are precious, but take the RISK! We know that you're passionate about the relationship, but please take the RISK because of the eternal consequences. Take the RISK, invite your world.

What does this do? It triggers followship. It simply starts the ball rolling. It mobilises people and gives them the space and scope to move in the direction the leaders are moving in.

Followship is triggered. People are birthed into this environment and followship becomes the norm.

Herman M. Koelliker says, "One man working with you is like a dozen men working for you."

Develop an evangelistic strategy.

1.8 I I Am Joseph

The reality is that if a leader is to be intentional in creating followship, then the leader has to give the followers something clear to follow. High on the agenda for church life in the 21st century is the pursuit and understanding of branding. Here at Breathe City Church we are very clinical and uncompromising regarding our Visual Standards Policy. We are active in ensuring that all our communications fit the branding that we believe is correct for the house. In fact, we are more intentional regarding our branding than people realise – even to the point of recognising that we are a "branded house" not a "house of brands". This means that all ministries and sectors, pastors and ministry directors, leaders and administrators all communicate what they have to say in alignment with our policy.

We have even trademarked Breathe City Church and its logo!

Why do I tell you this? Please follow me...

I now have the privilege of hosting many a church leader who comes and ask many questions regarding the seemingly swift growth of our church. Almost every leader asks questions about our branding and how to establish such a strong identity.

Every time I give the same answer: "Read James Allen's book first." (James' book, *As a Man Thinketh*, is a must read for any leader!)

The Bible gives us clear instructions on how to establish a brand. It states, *"As a man thinketh, so he is"* (Proverbs 23:7).

In order to give the church a clear identity that followers can identify, own and follow, a leader must communicate clearly "who" the church is. The leader must also be very clear on who they are also. Once we know who we are and can clearly communicate who we are, then we can trigger followship.

It all starts with how we think!

The story of Joseph is one of my all-time favourites. I often comment that RT Kendall's book, *God Meant it For Good*, was a game changer for me. It has been arguably one of the most definitive reads of my entire life thus far.

Just one sentence of Joseph's entire story exploded into my world with significant collateral effect – not only in terms of my personal revelation, but in how it went on to affect every area of our church and to this day continues to be one of the banks of our river.

(A river without banks is just a large puddle going nowhere. Strong banks give a river its strength, velocity and the ability to the reach the sea. Every church that wants to fulfil its mission must have strong river banks. I call them river banks. You may understand them as non-negotiables).

In Genesis 45:3 Joseph exclaims in a loud voice something that every leader needs to experience and have revelation of:

I AM JOSEPH!

Due to Joseph's prominent position at that time, word would have spread very quickly until the whole world heard these three powerful words.

OK, so I've built this up and obviously I now need to unpack the importance of this...

Joseph's story began in chapter 37 of Genesis. It takes another nine chapters (a prison, an accusation, a palace, a promotion, a recognition of being forgotten, a jealous family and much more in between) before Joseph cries out, "I AM JOSEPH!"

For us, I AM JOSEPH described a journey of becoming. Joseph always was Joseph, but a process of becoming had to take place. He could have made this declaration at any point during his story, but he didn't. First, he had to become! He had to go on a journey of becoming who he was destined to be. He had to discover who he really was.

As intentional leaders we have to go on a journey of becoming. We have to lead the church through a process of discovering who we really are, so that we can become who we are destined to become. Then we can build our communication, brand and activity in a strong and powerful way. That is why "I AM JOSPEH" is such a significant river bank for me and for our church. We know who we are and therefore we know what we should be doing … and not doing.

The reason why leaders struggle to create followship is that they are too random, too much like a big puddle, trying to be everything to everyone. In so doing they actually become nothing to a few. If you want to go on the journey of creating great followship, then it is imperative that you first journey to becoming!

The journey of becoming commences with a God moment. For Joseph it was a couple of dreams. Building church is a God thing; it's a spiritual thing and not a "good idea" thing. Many a leader and church, in my opinion, is never going to be a "grower" simply because it hasn't been birthed out of a God-moment – a dream, a call, a mandate, call it what you will.

Listen, for followship to be created it has to give followers something significant to follow. Jonathan knew, in the very depths of who he was, that it was never right to be sat under a pomegranate tree when there was an enemy to be taken out. This propelled him to provoke a response from his armour bearer. This in turn created followship as 600 soldiers and the Hebrews hiding in the caves saw and followed suit.

Note that Joseph didn't merely keep the God-moment to himself; he communicated it so much that it got him into deep trouble. The I AM JOSEPH revelation became a river bank for me and our church because the journey of becoming forces the river to go where it ought to go. Becoming who you are designed to be can sometimes isolate you from where you used to reside and bring you into where you are designed to reside. This is so important for intentional leaders trying to create followship. It actually defines who will follow.

Creating followship is more than getting a cool brand look. It's about knowing who you are, communicating that revelation and helping others who resonate with you to connect and go with you.

Part Two:
Followship Exists

2.1 | Further Defining Followship

The pattern of writing that works for me is that I go away for a few days and, at the end of each day, I upload the day's writing and my PA reads through it and texts me some thoughts to help and assist. This morning as I sit to write, a text comes through stating that the word "followship" shows up on Microsoft Word as a typing error. The word followship has little red dots underneath it, implying that it is a spelling mistake.

Followship, as a word, doesn't exist.

That's why this book is hard to write and needs to be written. For great church to be established we know that leadership is essential, but we also need something that doesn't exist!

Can I push this analogy further?

Hopefully we all agree that the armour bearer's activity is a vital example to us all, but according to the English language there isn't a single descriptive word that encompasses and allows us to understand this activity. So we're creating a new word.

Followship.

Every new word needs to be defined.

Psalm 23 is possibly one of the most famous of all passages of Scripture. Through school and Kids Church I was taught to memorise it and throughout my ministerial life I have constantly referred to it.

I am seeing it in a new light as I have been preparing to write this book, however.

Psalm 23 is a psalm that maps out what followship looks like. It shows the heart, the passion, the standard and the results of followship.

"The LORD is my shepherd;
I have all that I need.
He lets me rest in green meadows;
he leads me beside peaceful streams.
He renews my strength.
He guides me along right paths,
bringing honour to his name.
Even when I walk
through the darkest valley,
I will not be afraid,
for you are close beside me.
Your rod and your staff
protect and comfort me.
You prepare a feast for me
in the presence of my enemies.
You honour me by anointing my head with oil.
My cup overflows with blessings.
Surely your goodness and unfailing love will pursue me
all the days of my life,
and I will live in the house of the LORD forever."

Six verses that help us to understand followship.

"The Lord is my shepherd; I have all I need" is a statement of recognition that we are being shepherded. It acknowledges the fact that we need a shepherd and then clearly demonstrates contentment in that revelation. Yes, I know that David is writing about his relationship with his Heavenly Father, but another name for pastor is shepherd. Pastors shepherd.

When training pastors we very often look at the Old Testament model of a shepherd to help them understand what it is to pastor people. But as followers we can look at the same scripture and learn how to be "shepherded" – to learn what it is to be a great follower. I am recognising more and more that the better at followship a person is, the more content they are.

The second verse talks about how the sheep are happy to be led into green meadows and alongside peaceful streams. Two things stand out here. The first is that the shepherd or pastor isn't someone we merely run to when we're having a tough time. Their leadership and guidance is just as present in the lush and peaceful times.

The volume of pastors I have coming to me saying how busy they are amazes me. Looking at their time sheets it is easy to see why. They are being pulled to and fro by the demands of the people.

Followship doesn't look like this.

Followship understands that the shepherd has somewhere to go and simply follows. The sheep aren't asking the shepherd to go to the field that they want to go to, or to follow the stream they prefer; the sheep are happy to be led where the shepherd leads them.

In this psalm David is showing us that He is following his shepherd and because of his followship he is therefore experiencing rest in green meadows and walks by peaceful streams. He is going somewhere and enjoying it.

Followship is not meant to be difficult – it is a pleasant experience.

Verse 3 is significant. The phrase "renews my strength" gives me the strongest indication that followship is SO not about "cloning" or getting people to do what the leader wants, but absolutely about empowering people to walk along "right paths" which in turn brings "glory to His name". I am convinced that we have understood what it is to follow through tainted experiences and hurt eyes. We have been fearful because of bad leadership, top-heavy leadership, manipulative leadership. But significant and successful churches that scatter seed and see more than the 25% harvest – and are moving more towards a 100% harvest – have two contributing strengths: Great Leadership AND Great Followship. They work hand in hand. We will address this idea more later.

Verse 4 shows what should be the intimate side of the relationship between leaders and followers. Even when I'm walking through the darkest valley in life (and we know life has some dark valleys) this verse tells me that the shepherd is close by. Leaders and followers alike have to eradicate the institutional perceptions that grip the Church. This is organic, relational, a process of doing life together. We're with each other. It isn't merely about coming to meetings on a Sunday. It's about the journey of life.

Verse 5 gives a hint that this followship dimension produces great victory and anointing. Of course it does, we're aligning ourselves as followers with a leader's vision and together victory comes. We all talk of Psalm 133, about how dwelling together in unity causes the blessing to come. It is evidenced here in Psalm 23 also.

In today's terms we have Synergy and Collaboration, but Scripture captured this way earlier.

Followship is biblical!

Finally, verse 6 gives us a greater dimension to observe. It's about longevity. I understand that life takes people in different directions, but for a follower to really see substantial fruit "all the days of my life," longevity has to be significantly examined. As a generation we are so quick to make demands, but an overview of church life says that Leaders and Followers who have been together and journeyed together over the years, even decades, see a far greater harvest than flash-in-the-pan experiences.

At Breathe City Church we recognise that we have only been together for 4 years. Yes, we are now approaching 1,000 people, but we've only been going 4 years.

Yet, there are many leadership/followship relationships at BCC which have stood the test of time and experience. We will look at some of these later.

In addition, we are very much aware that the fruit of what has happened in the last 4 years will only truly be seen in the next 20 or so years. That is why we are so aware of intentionality. In 20 year's time we want to see that fruit, the harvest, the abundance that we are believing for.

2.2 | Different Types of Followship

For a number of years I played golf. I had always wanted to play, but never really had the opportunity. However, whilst I lived in Cardiff I got the opportunity for about seven years to play. I took lessons and joined a club. What I never realised was how many different levels of official "buy-in" are available at a golf club: five day members, weekend members, full members, veteran members, juniors, off-peak only members, even guest membership which gave you a 20% reduction in green fees only!

What I further discovered is that once you've chosen your level of buy-in (depending on how eager you are, how good you become and how often you attend) your role and activity in the club can become so great that you become "part of the scene" or a "proper golfer".

By the end of my golfing years I was a +7 handicapper, a fully-fledged member, even team captain. I was on the sub-committee and I even got to be involved at board level in discussions about the sale of the club to new owners.

All voluntary.

All enjoyed.

It's the same in church.

In life.

It's the same in regard to followship.

As a lead pastor I know that there are people who "buy-in" at whatever level they choose to. Like the golf club though, to enjoy the benefits of the club and experience what it is to be a golfer, there has to be some level of buy-in.

The institutional, historic aspect of church as merely a place we turn up to at 11.00am on a Sunday is archaic. It doesn't exist any more. Instead, people need to discover their level of buy-in.

This is followship!

Leadership has to map out what people can buy-in to. The vision isn't merely a statement that sounds nice – it's a flag of intent. It says, "This is what we see and this is where we're heading ... do you want in?"

People come to BCC not because it's a great church, which it is, but because it's a great journey! They are getting on board with something exciting and adventurous. People choose their level of buy-in.

This is an unofficial buy-in list that I have observed:

Vision Catchers

The first level of followship is being a Vision Catcher. This simply means being a person who "gets" the vision. They have caught it. It has caught them, their interest, their imagination. The days of turning up for church on a Sunday for appearance's sake are gone. People want to belong. They look for where the leaders are going and ask themselves, "Do I want to belong? Do I want to get on that ship?"

This is why it is essential for leaders to be going somewhere. It is also essential for leaders to be communicating where they are going and it is essential that they have a high delivery quota when it comes to vision, because followers need to see vision fulfilled.

Followers are designed to follow. Intentionality says, "Get real good at communicating vision and delivering." My friend Gary Smith, who runs Ignite in South Wales, constantly tells his staff to "promise little and deliver big" – great advice to leaders. Stop promising the world and start delivering on what you promise!

Vision Carers

The second level of followship is being a Vision Carer. These people buy-in at a more intense level because they do more than simply get the vision. It is more than simply "of interest" to them. Yes, it captures their imagination, but they also care about its fulfilment. Vision Carers exhibit the qualities of Matthew 7:20:

"Just as you can identify a tree by its fruit, so you can identify people by their actions..."

You know when people are Vision Carers ... because they care. When you care for something, you look after it, protect it and consider it. Vision Carers do more than just get the vision, they take care of the vision. Vision Carers live in such a way that they will never damage the vision.

This means that they don't get in the way, but are actually a part of the vision. They look like the vision!

The vision of Breathe City Church is to "build a church that loves people for who they are and inspires them to become all that they can be". Vision Carers are people who are being built into people who love people for who they are and who inspire people to become all that they can be. The vision is seen in their activity. It is who they are. They are BCC! This is a concept we will wrestle with later.

Vision Carriers

"Where your treasure is, there your heart is also" (Luke 12:34) best illustrates a Vision Carrier. Oh yes, they have caught the vision and for sure they care for the vision, but this level of buy-in is SO much more and is again easy to identify.

When people in church are giving financially, giving of their time and efforts, releasing their skills into the life of the house, pastoring others, serving others and living for others, then it is evident that they are carrying the vision. These are the people who "buy-in" at such a level that their followship is an example to others. It is their followship that is facilitating the vision. It is their followship that is actually making the vision become a reality! These people carry the vision. They are working towards making the vision become a reality.

Vision Casters

Vision Casters are at the ultimate level of buy-in. Not only do they catch the vision; not only do they care for the vision; they even go beyond carrying the vision. Vision Casters are the ones whose followship is so clear that others follow them! It is their followship that facilitates the followship of others. Their whole lives cast the vision. They communicate the vision even when they are saying nothing.

Part of the culture at BCC is the core value of honour our Vision Casters have. It was Rhi Davies (a Vision Caster) who pulled all the staff team together to work on a strategy of introducing practical steps that could model honour so that honour could be tangibly seen across the life of the church. It was this Vision Caster who then gathered the Ministry Directors and Pastors together to explain what the staff were doing. Now people clearly see honour as an identifiable part of our culture. They see it because people have bought in at such a level that they cast vision that others catch, care for and carry.

The issue and level of buy-in is something we need to intentionally work with.

2.3 | Selecting Leaders of Followship

Now that we have some understanding of what followship is and its differing levels of buy-in, we have to address the issue of selecting leaders who will help with the process of followship.

Once again, the story of Jonathan and his armour bearer is relevant.

It actually gives us four insights into how best to select the right people for the job.

Jonathan was full of vision. He saw. Scripture doesn't say when this vision initially came. All we know is that at a certain point in history, he spoke of his desire to *"go over to where the Philistines have their outpost."* The first insight into selecting leaders of followship then, is this: **who heard you?** We see here that the armour bearer responded, meaning that he had heard Jonathan.

When Jesus said, *"I will build my church,"* He said it to Peter, who had previously answered Jesus' question regarding who He was by stating, *"You are the Messiah, the son of the living God."* Peter heard Jesus. Yes, he saw Him too, but Peter heard the question being asked. The armour bearer heard the "defiant intent" of Jonathan.

The first port of call is to select people who "hear" the leader. This is really important. Don't select people who hear what they want to hear. Think about the 600 soldiers and the Hebrews hiding in the caves. Think about what would have happened if the armour bearer had heard something different to what Jonathan said. Think about the collateral damage that could have occurred if they had climbed the hill to the Philistines and the armour bearer had heard his own agenda rather that what Jonathan had envisioned – it would have been a catastrophe!

Remember this: leaders have influence. Therefore, when selecting leaders of followship, ensure that they are people who have heard the leader, heard the vision, heard the heart!

The second thing regarding selecting leaders of followship is simply to **ensure that an armour bearer is selected**! Now, you may frown, but Jonathan was Saul's son. He could have selected anybody to be with him, but he selected an armour bearer. We know that God can use a donkey to speak if He has to. We also know that God selected a cup bearer in Nehemiah. But Jonathan, in pursuing his vision, selected an armour bearer.

It is essential this is understood. In the heat of the battle against the Philistines the armour bearer would have been unswerving in his loyalty to Jonathan. The armour bearer's role was one of absolute commitment. He was an armour bearer: one equipped to bear arms. There is a tendency in leadership to select from those people who are charismatic, those who are talented, but Jonathan selected the one who had character, resilience and was at his side.

Intentionality lesson: *followship is only developed through trust and solidarity.*

In the heat of the battle, 600 soldiers and the Hebrews hiding in caves followed two men together against all the odds. They saw the bravery and commitment of the armour bearer alongside Jonathan and that was the example they followed.

Select armour bearers!

The third thing we can observe here is that **the armour bearer was of a positive disposition**. Don't select cold water pourers. Select people who consider impossible to be nothing. Think about the armour bearer for one moment. He knew the responsibility that he carried. To be the armour bearer to Jonathan – that is as serious as it gets! There was no way that the armour bearer was returning from this excursion without Jonathan. If Jonathan got killed and he had to return to Saul with the news, then he was a dead man anyway. He knew that the implications of this adventure could cost him his life. Therefore, he was a guy who was going to make this thing happen.

Vision is fulfilled when armour bearers and Jonathans refuse to believe that it won't happen. The fulfilment of vision occurs when people refuse to be dictated to by opposition and obstacles. Select overcomers, people with a "yes" mindset; people with a "whatever it takes" paradigm.

The final, potentially the most important, and quite possibly the most dangerous key is to **select an armour bearer who will model what is required for the vision to be fulfilled**! Let me explain.

When the 600 soldiers and the Hebrews hiding in caves saw Jonathan and the armour bearer, they were inspired and followed the example that was set.

Select people who will set the example that is required.

Does the person look like the vision fulfilled? Does the person have what it takes to model that which is required to see the fulfilment of the vision? If they aren't the embodiment of what is required to best model it to others, then don't select them. Remember the buy-ins to vision: Vision Catchers, Carers, Carriers and Casters. If people are catching a vision of something and it doesn't look like the fulfilment of your vision, then they won't be caring, carrying or casting your vision either.

This is huge.

Let's drill a little deeper. We can unpack this further by saying we need to select people who are "heart and soul" with the leader. The reply of the armour bearer of, "I'm with you heart and soul" implies that people may be with us in their soul, but not in their heart! Think intentionally for a moment ... the armour bearer will be the example to the 600 soldiers and the Hebrews hiding in caves. Jonathans must select "heart and soul" people. Put another way, they must be people whose hearts and souls are with Jonathan. In other words, not merely people who are with the leader in their heart, but people who actually get what this vision is all about. If a person of heart is selected, but ultimately they don't "get it", then eventually it will strain the relationship. If a person totally gets it, but their heart is not with Jonathan, then what is required will not happen because there is too great a cost.

2.4 | Caught and Taught

In my last book I briefly mentioned something that occurs in the process of repurposing. I talked of the response of people to change and the leader's responsibility to ensure that culture is established. I talk of Caught, Taught or Sort as the three obvious avenues of activity. However, leading change is very different to leading progress...

There does come a stage in a church or leader's activity where the "sort" aspect becomes irrelevant as people now know who the leader is and what the church stands for. The vision is clear so people can choose to be a part of it or not. The "sort" therefore is default. In the context of understanding and developing followship, "caught" and "taught" are hugely important.

Caught

Jonathan speaks to his armour bearer and, as previously stated, the armour bearer doesn't even ask for the vision to be explained. He simply buys in straight away. This is what is known as "caught". The armour bearer catches the spirit of Jonathan and his vision in an instant.

This happens.

Excellent followship is easily recognised and most sought after. A leader casts vision and a person instantly catches it, cares for it, carries it and then even casts that same vision. It is in their DNA; it is a miraculous thing to behold. It is my observation that, actually, most leaders only lead those who catch their vision or spirit. They are the easy ones. It happens so wonderfully that the obvious question is asked: Why can't everyone be like that?

The reality is that not everyone is called to be like that and, as a footnote, any leader who merely runs the easy route is never going to see vision fulfilled.

Yes, it is essential for a certain number of people to catch the vision – to catch the spirit of the leader. The armour bearer caught the vision. He caught the spirit of Jonathan and instantly was ready for that which lay ahead. There doesn't seem to be any training required, little conversation is had. It seems that the story didn't take place over years, but moments – so this process happened in a very short space of time. We, in our natural thinking, struggle to get our heads round how quickly this can happen. But we all know that it does.

Always look out for those who catch the vision and the spirit of a leader. They will always be an armour bearer. It's their calling!

Taught

The majority of your people, however, will not respond in the same way as the armour bearer and this is what I want to address. Leaders want the response of the masses to be like that of the armour bearer. Leaders cast vision and expect the whole congregation to embrace it with open arms, with no questions or concerns, and then run towards fulfilling it. Since this generally doesn't happen, however, the work load is placed on the Jonathans and the armour bearers and therefore the vision is generally left unfulfilled. Jonathan and his armour bearer, on their own, don't have all that is required to bring the fulfilment. As a result, people get frustrated and burn out happens. Jonathan quits and his armour bearer is left wondering what he has just given his life to and what is he to do now. I think this is what is evidenced when we see church failing.

Have a look at 1 Samuel 14 again and take some encouragement from being intentional in designing great followship.

Jonathan and the armour bearer, who has caught the vision and spirit of his leader, set out and climbed the hill. Then they engaged with the enemy in dialogue and then they engaged in ferocious fighting.

That is what is happening in the story looked at from one perspective. This is the perspective we most expect to see in church life. Let's look from another perceptive.

The 600 soldiers are sat under the pomegranate tree.

In comfort.

They have all the resources for warfare, but they are sat under a pomegranate tree. As they scan the horizon they see two figures rise before them and one soldier says to another, "What's going on there?" The other says, "Oh, I read about this, it's called warfare." The first soldier replies, "Isn't that what we are supposed to do?"

Many people in churches are watching. They have heard stories about great churches and about great vision being fulfilled and are very excited to read about them. Deep down, they know they have what it takes to be involved with something equally spectacular, but they have only read about it. They have never seen it modelled or exampled. So they continue to sit under the pomegranate tree while two people engage with the enemy. And with no help, or without God's intervention, those two people are done for.

What happens in 1 Samuel 14 is that Jonathan and the armour bearer behave in such a way that the soldiers get a model. Jonathan and the armour bearer are so inspirational in their pursuit of the vision that it causes 600 soldiers to be roused from their comfort. The former generation of Saul doesn't quite get it, but insists that they have to be a part of it, and even those hiding have grasped that they no longer have to live in fear. So more and more come alongside the 600 soldiers in their followship of Jonathan the armour bearer.

The key here is to understand that the 600 soldiers wanted to be a part of this, but they were too far away from the conversation to catch it. They needed to be taught it. Intentional leadership decides to work tirelessly in providing great models and explanations for as many people as possible.

Put the armour bearers on show who are exampling what it is to be in victory. Highlight the mum who is doing really well with her kids. Showcase the guy who got the promotion at work and ask him to explain in follower terms how it came to pass. Direct people's attention to the new leader who has developed so fast and draw people's focus to the journey he has been on. Flag up the people making decisions to follow Jesus and paint their story on huge canvases for people to see! Then, armour bearing behaviour becomes the norm. It sets the example for the 600 soldiers and the Hebrews in hiding to follow ... and they will!

2.5 | Paul and Intentionality

Continuing our journey of exploring followship, let's turn our attention to scriptural examples of how intentional a leader can be in creating great followship.

I love reading the letters from Paul. The guy is a hero of mine. The parts of the Bible he wrote lay the foundation for much of what we know about how we are to be as church. However, have you ever read his letters from the perspective of what he is doing rather than what he is saying?

For instance, we know that Paul dealt with many things in many churches. We see the church in Corinth get a slap and we see the church in Ephesus get massaged with a message! We see Paul train some great young pastors such as Titus and Timothy.

Let's look at Paul and how he intentionally writes to Timothy – who is a great leader in his own right, but that stems from his ability to be a great follower. The other week I put a tweet out: if you make a lousy follower, then you'll make a lousy leader.

Great followship stems from intentional leaders training people who follow to lead well, causing more and better followers.

The first thing I wish to highlight about how Paul writes to Timothy is how many times Paul writes or mentions himself. I mean it's all about Jesus right? And yes, we know that Paul once said, *"Follow me as I follow Christ"* (1 Corinthians 11:1). But come on, it is all about Jesus! Read the letters from Paul to Timothy again.

In mentoring and discipling Timothy, Paul uses himself as the example. He understood that followers best follow with something in front of them. I'm not going to quote all the times that Paul says, "I" because I want you, the reader, to examine this for yourself. Paul uses "I" a lot!

What is happening here?

The first thing is, as already stated, Paul is giving Timothy a physical and practical example using himself. The second and most important thing is deeper and more intentional. Paul knows that Timothy is a leader. Paul is training Timothy, under the radar, to train other followers. He is using himself as an example for Timothy and he is giving Timothy an example of how best to be an example.

The second thing I see (and this occurs throughout Paul's writing) is how Paul tackles the "elephant in the room". I love how Paul sets the standard for choosing elders and deacons. He doesn't make it easy to build church. He is bold enough to raise Timothy's expectations of what leadership and governance should look like. When he talks of deacons (those who serve) he never mentions using people who are available. He never lowers the bar. He sets it. In Timothy's learning, he learns at a high standard.

Intentionality says, "Don't be afraid to set the bar regarding the standard that is expected of followers." It is there for those who will model how to live for other followers.

A third thing that should be highlighted is that Paul keeps it simple. I mean, really! Look at what he talks about to Timothy: errors of doctrine and false teachers, how to behave in corporate worship, he lists Timothy's responsibilities ("cling to your faith in Christ"), leadership and what it looks like in church, the requirements of leaders, more stuff on false teachers, advising widows, elders and slaves (how to help people get on in life)... and he finishes 1 Timothy by once again highlighting the issue of dodgy teaching and avoiding godless and foolish discussions.

Intentional leaders keep things really simple. They don't beat about the bush, they say it like it is.

Don't waste words. Just say what needs to be said. Communicate what needs to be communicated.

It really is that simple. We complicate things so much. We build apologies and excuses into everything out of a concern that our followers won't get it.

They will. Keep it simple.

The final thing that I will highlight or re-emphasise is similar to what I have previously written. 1 Timothy. Then 2 Timothy. Pretty much the same thing. Go on read it. Yes, there are some additions, but in general Paul repeats what he has already stated: keep on track, keep going and watch out for dodgy, false doctrine and teachers. Paul is very intentional in continuing to bang the same drum. Leaders should continually be banging the same drum. Leaders, preachers in particular, are always looking for the latest revelation, gimmick or story – which is all good, but when you have been around for a while it begins to dawn on you that Ecclesiastes 1:9 is right: there is nothing new under the sun.

Come on, think about it. God is still banging the same drum several thousand years later and He is the Creator! We may need to say things differently, but let's make sure the message is plain and clear so that followers know what they are following.

This may seem a little flippant, but what I'm attempting to do is to strip away the complications we have placed around leadership and challenge us all to make it easy for people to follow. Great followship occurs when followers are empowered to follow. They genuinely want to; they are designed to and called to. We are all called to follow and lead at some level. So let's make it easier for ourselves.

Now let's ground this a little so we can hear something.

The message is still the same, but we can be very intentional in how we communicate it, so that followship occurs more readily.

On the next page is an example of intentionality.

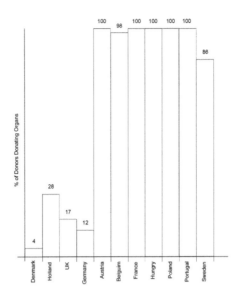

Why are there two very clear different outcomes to these results? Are some countries more caring than others?

Is it to do with insurance or culture or religion or affluence? No.

It is to do with intentionality.

The first section people were presented with:

"Check the box below if you want to participate in the organ donor programme."

The second section people were presented with:

"Check the box below if you don't want to participate in the organ donor programme."

The difference is immense. Let's get intentional with our leadership in creating great followship. Paul did it and it seems as though donor programmes in places like Austria, Belgium, France, Hungary, Poland, Portugal and Sweden did it too!

2.6 | The Law of Innovation

You will have heard it said that there is a lot we can learn from the business community. I am going to show you that the business community truly does understand that followship exists and has also grasped the philosophy of this understanding, using it to its advantage. It is especially apparent in its advertising and evidenced by its bottom line.

Apple is a genius at this.

Please hear me, after you have read the following, I will repeat the same using totally different words and phrases but it will have the same conclusion. The following example will be corporate, but then I will use Scripture to show that the business community has grasped something that the New Testament teaches, though we are sometimes too religious and boxed into our paradigms to see it.

The business community is extremely aware of what is known as "The Law of Innovation", first presented by Ev Rogers, which places people in different categories that define how businesses will communicate to them as they target these different groups with their advertising.

The product that is being sold here is not the "be all and end all" of the equation. In fact, companies that have a leading product have often dramatically failed to succeed with it because they targeted the wrong group or type of people.

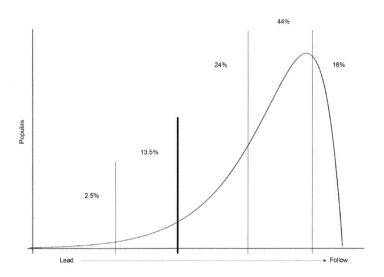

When looking at the graph, it kind of makes sense to go after the largest section of people. The largest section is the 24% and 44%. Mass marketing, mass communication, get the word out there, let's hit as many people as possible. It is a proven fact that this way of doing business generally draws a blank. Occasionally, it may make a score, but in general the Law of Innovation is called a "law" because it doesn't break.

Look again at the graph in the light of the following descriptions of the percentages/people types.

2.5% of people are *Innovators*. These are the people who go first; make it happen; create something out of nothing. These are the people you want on your staff. These are the FANTASTIC people who seem to ooze creativity and innovation.

13.5% of people are what can be described as *Early Adopters*. These are the FANTASTIC people that latch onto things real quick. They are the type of people who are ahead of the curve. They see what's happening and get on board with the agenda, create the trend and lead the way.

24% of people see what is happening and then get on board. They aren't so much trend setters as *Trend Followers*. They will be wearing the latest label or carrying the latest gadget, but they will have seen someone else doing so first. They wouldn't be brave enough to go out on a limb, but when they see others doing it, they buy in.

44% of people are a lot slower. Don't get me wrong, they'll make sure that they get the latest gadget or designer jeans, but they'll wait 'til Christmas or get it in the sale. They don't look out of place or anything, but they don't really see what's happening until it's really happening and then they arrange to jump on the band wagon. They most definitely aren't trend followers, but when a trend is established they'll buy in.

16% of people are what can be described as *Laggers*. They lag so far behind that it is painfully obvious. These are the people who have just realised that it's 2012 and that Top of the Pops is no longer on BBC 1 on Friday nights. These are the people who have just got themselves an email address and have stopped wearing Kickers. The business community wastes little time and resource here.

What the business community has learnt is that there is a solid wall that must be scaled before breakthrough comes. The solid wall is found at the pinnacle of the early adopters. 13.5% and 24% are two very different sections. The 24% don't arrive on the scene until the innovators and early adopters have gathered momentum.

What the business community has discovered is that the bulk of society (the 24% and 44% sections) don't know how to function, purchase, operate or even dress themselves without the innovators and early adopters leading the way. Due to this finding, companies like Apple actively pursue FANTASTIC people. They look to employ innovators and engage with early adopters. Their communication and marketing is slick, simplistic and specifically designed to trigger the early adopters. They know that the early adopters will be on their front foot and be camped outside their stores in the freezing cold, simply to get hold of their newest device.

They also know that early adopters are fiercely brand loyal. Therefore they look not only to sell them a product, but engage with them in a far more personal way. It's more than getting their email address and post code, it's about allowing them to feel part of a community that they can belong to and add value to.

They have also discovered that early adopters are the best form of marketing going. Once this type of person is on side, they are very public in their support and applause.

What do "trend-followers" follow?

Trend?

No!

They follow "trend-setters"!

People always follow people.

The business world has learnt something very powerful. The Law of Innovation is a proven law that lends itself to the concept of leadership and followship. It adds strength to the understanding of leading intentionally and not randomly hoping things will work. If business leaders operated in the random and hopeful way that church leaders have been accustomed to, they'd be fired by their board.

Let's unpack this a little further by looking at the same discussion from biblical context. Like I said earlier, I think that the business world has learnt something that is hidden in Scripture, but because of a religious mindset, the Church has had a restricted view of what the New Testament is revealing about leadership and followship.

2.7 | #GoGetTheFANTASTICPeople

The reality is that even though the previous section makes absolute sense, as the Church we still have a commitment to the "whosoever" and therefore we struggle with being so ruthlessly specific in pursuing the innovators and the early adopters. Yes, we fully grasp the concept of Jonathan and his armour bearer, but we perceive that New Testament ideology directs us to the "harvest field" not the isolated person.

I put it to you that, even though there is a harvest field that needs harvesting, the New Testament actually reveals a strategy that not only affirms the Law of Innovation, but actually promotes the pursuit of a person, not a crowd.

I stumbled across Deuteronomy 32:30 which highlights the principle that 2 can chase 10,000. Many a "churches together" forum has used this to highlight the importance of unity. Can I direct your attention to the fact that the same verse informs us that 1 can chase 1,000? We sometimes miss this.

ONE
Can
Chase
1,000.

The important thing here is our perception of ONE. We pursue the crowd because we fail to understand the potential of ONE.

Acts 9 tells the epic story of Saul's conversion.

I have preached on it several times, but always failed to realise that the story is about Saul.

ONE person...

...whom God pursued.

Yes, God had the harvest field in mind. He sent his ONE and only Son for the "whosoever" and here He says, *"Go, for Saul is my chosen instrument to take my message to the Gentiles."* God went after the ONE. What fascinates me even more is that this pattern of pursuing ONE person is replicated time and time again throughout the New Testament. We see Paul himself follow this strategy when, in Acts 16, embarking on his second missionary journey, he pursues ONE:

"Paul went first to Derbe and then to Lystra, where there was a young disciple named Timothy. His mother was a Jewish believer, but his father was a Greek. Timothy was well thought of by the believers in Lystra and Iconium, so Paul wanted him to join them on their journey."

Please see this: God went after ONE in Saul. Paul went after ONE in Timothy. It gets even more fascinating. The ONE wasn't any old ONE, but actually the ONE was a FANTASTIC person. Saul was the best of the best, being FANTASTIC in his pursuit of the Church. Timothy was extremely well thought of and had great credibility. To break down a religious mindset here... I believe that the New Testament teaches us to go after the FANTASTIC individuals that we believe can help leaders fulfil their mission. They can even be FANTASTIC people who are far away from God. I don't think you can be further away from God than Saul was. Or the FANTASTIC people can be in other churches, even other cities, such as Timothy. I know this raises the whole "sheep stealing" issue, but I will address that later.

I believe our strategy should be to go and find the FANTASTIC people who will function as armour bearers to the Jonathans. Psalm 2:8 says, *"Ask of me and I will make the nations your inheritance..."* I would be bold as to say that I'm not yet asking for the nations, simply the FANTASTIC people who are called to walk this adventure with me and build a great church in my home city. I believe every leader has God-given FANTASTIC people that they should be praying in and pursuing – and then intentionally attracting them to understand their armour bearing role.

Instantly I can hear the reaction of established paradigms uttering phrases such as, "That is elitist" or "That doesn't sound Christlike." I beg to differ. I think Jesus Himself operated with a Go Get The FANTASTIC People strategy.

Not only did Jesus hand pick 12 young men to disciple, train and equip to change the world, He also trained people he sent on mission to have the same strategy. When I read Luke 10 where Jesus sends out the 72, in differing translations and digging into the direction of what Jesus is instructing, I see a clear alignment with the pursuit of ONE; the pursuit of the FANTASTIC person. Jesus instructs the 72 to go and discover "the man of peace"; the key to the community; the ONE who will open his home, community, even city. Jesus did preach to the crowds, but always challenged the ONEs.

Jesus also tells the Parable of the Talents where, I think, He allows us to see this paradigm at work in a bigger setting. Matthew 25 is a powerful chapter that should challenge every leader regarding stewardship, intentionality, diligence and effective ministry to the world around us. This chapter haunts me and I often refer to it as the "MATT25CHALLENGE". The whole chapter engages the reader in how a person relates to and serves people. The Parable of the Talents is, I believe, not about how we handle our money (yet we can read it in that isolated context), but more about how we handle that which the Master gives us. The rest of the chapter seems to be directing our attention to our involvement with people. I believe the Parable of the Talents, from a leadership perspective, is challenging a leader regarding how the people, as followers, are utilised.

Please allow me the liberty of unpacking this.

Just like the parable, to some a multiple of 5 is given, while others receive 2 and some receive 1. Don't ask me why some get more than others. The reality is, the answer to that is above my pay scale. What I see though, is that the Master entrusts more to some than to others. To those who fully utilise that which is placed in their hand, a doubling occurs. Note here, if leaders fully utilise the people in their followship, then a doubling occurs. If a leader wants a church to grow, then they must fully grasp the Ephesians 4 understanding that our job is to *"equip the saints for works of service"*. Church grows when saints perform "works of service". Empower, mobilise and equip followers and watch church grow – even double.

Yet note this: When what is in our hand is not utilised, it is taken away with rebuke and given to the one who fully utilised that which was in their hand. My bold, even audacious trail of thought takes me to Paul and the pursuit of Timothy. It is my incredibly edgy belief that as I commit to utilising that which is in my hand, equipping followers, then even that which is not in my hand (or rather who) will be taken from elsewhere and placed with me. That means people who potentially could be in other churches, if they are not fully utilised and are called to walk with me, will one day be placed with me. Therefore, I may not yet be asking for the nations, but I am most certainly asking God to release to me those who are called to walk with me: the FANTASTIC people!

#GoGetTheFANTASTICPeople.

2.8 | Leadership is Visual

As we have seen from Jonathan and his relationship with his armour bearer, and now Paul and his relationship with Timothy: a great leader is paramount to creating great followers.

The intentionality of this process is hopefully becoming clearer as we progress through this book. The next section of the book is more practical in helping leaders be intentional in creating great followship, but before we begin that section I think it would be helpful to highlight one more area.

Jonathan did speak to his armour bearer and Paul did write to Timothy, but I am more aware of the physicality of their communication. As mentioned, Paul wrote to Timothy and spoke about himself a lot in the process, even using himself as an example. Jonathan spoke to his armour bearer, but they both ascended the hill to engage with the enemy.

As a generation we recognise that we are visually stimulated more than any other. Millions of images are beamed into our view every day and we are plagued with advertising wherever we look. There are messages being communicated to us all the time and those message are made to look as attractive and appealing as possible.

The leader needs to understand that for a person to catch their vision, to care, even to carry and possibly cast that vision, a very clear vision needs to be communicated. Yes, we can write it down and yes, we can constantly find ways of advancing it through ever changing media. But as human beings, the clearest way in which we will see that vision is by observing it in the people we follow. Jesus said, "Follow me." Paul said, "Follow me." Gideon said, "Follow me" and leaders must say, "Follow me."

It is imperative that leaders understand that the best way they can communicate the vision or message is to be a living representation of that vision or message. When God the Father wanted to tell the world how much He loved it, He did so by sending His Son – the message of His love incarnate.

Leaders have to be the vision. Leadership is visual.

There are so many messages being thrown around in the view of followers. To ensure that their vision is seen and caught, leaders must be very intentional.

Say "Thank you"

Leaders, church leaders in particular, are really good at saying "Please!" Leaders are very clever at getting people to do things that sometimes they don't like doing. We aren't talking about merely getting people to do things, we are intentionally leading people to a place where they catch, care, carry and even cast the vision. We are therefore attempting to empower people to be the vision themselves. One of the ways that this can be stimulated is to say, "Thank you." You may frown, but the reality is that in church life, "Thank you" is not often heard.

Red Bull was one of the first organisations to start the development of the thank you. Most brands focus on attracting attention by people coming. Red Bull began to understand that sending people works more effectively. If you went to an event that Red Bull was sponsoring, you would receive a complimentary drink on your way home. They knew that to leave you with something would make a significant impact.

We've been doing it at children's parties for centuries. Children come with a present for the birthday boy or girl, but on their departure goodie bags are distributed. Sometimes I wonder if my boys go to parties for the party or simply for the goodie bag!

Saying, "Thank you" has the same effect. It leaves a person with a sense of fulfilment, feeling that they have contributed to the success or fulfilment of the vision. Due to the amount of "noise" being created in the 21st Century, make sure the "Thank you" is loud and clear enough for people to hear. The effect of saying "Thank You" after an event or sending a letter to say, "Thank you" makes such an impact on followship.

Exaggerate Encouragement

It isn't merely achievement that excites people.

It isn't merely being involved in a project.

It is the time spent with people.

We are designed to be with other people. It feels so right because it is so right. The armour bearer was with Jonathan and when the 600 soldiers and Hebrews hiding in the caves saw the lead, they followed. However, be assured of this: first 1, then 2, then 10, then 100, then 600, and finally everyone got involved. Leadership was followed and followship was created, but it was only created as momentum occurred. This happens because encouragement is contagious. We all know that as children we would "egg one another on" to do things. The Bible tells the Church to, "spur one another on" (Hebrews 10:24). Encouragement creates followship.

Exaggerate the encouragement so that it can be seen.

Jonathan and his armour bearer were doing no small thing and it was seen. It encouraged others. I imagine as I play this scenario out in my mind that as the 600 soldiers and Hebrews who were hiding in the caves started to approach the battle scene, a war cry would have gone up. This is simply to exaggerate encouragement. Leaders, learn to cheer people on. Followers will latch on to this and do the same.

What will be heard and seen in the distance will be a war cry!

I hope that you, the reader, are discovering that followship can be created. Followship happens in its infancy with those who simply catch your vision. But intentional leadership realises that the crowd can be taught it if we think ahead and strategise. The next section begins to give practical strategies and examples of intentionally creating followship.

Part Three:
Establishing Followship

3.1 | Creating Buzz

In the first section of this book I began to introduce the concept that we have lost sight of something very important when it comes to building church. Yes, we know the importance of leadership, but there is another very important ingredient. That ingredient, we went on to say, was followship.

In the second section I began to unpack and define what followship is. Since it's a word that doesn't exist in the English language, we needed to explore its essential meaning and characteristics. We can see through Scripture, however, that followship is very real and very much part of Jesus' intention when building church.

In this third section I want now to address how followship is established. We identified that it is, at times, missing. But we now know what followship is and can now turn to the real issue of causing it to become a reality.

We will draw out *eight key components* of establishing followship. These eight components don't happen naturally or without external intervention in a church or organisation, so the leader has to be very intentional.

When I lived in Cardiff I had the immense privilege of working with thousands of young people across the city and region. Part of our operation was working in many of the senior schools. The concept was to be an aide to the school and a novelty resource that the teachers could draw on. Our programme was designed to work alongside the school curriculum and therefore we were able to work in individual schools several times a year and were seen as a benefit to the academic programme. The benefit to us was that we were then able to build long lasting relationships with the young people and thus we saw many lives changed by Jesus over a decade of youth ministry.

When we first started going into the schools, especially the hardened inner city schools, it was significantly noticed that we were the "outsiders". Actually, in some schools the atmosphere was quite intimidating. But after reading the story of the faith of the Centurion (Matthew 8:1-17) I began to grasp the revelation that, actually, I had the authority to be in that school. My paradigm shifted from me simply going into the school to me having the authority to set the atmosphere – in other words, that the young people were coming into my classroom or assembly hall. It began to dawn on me and then the team that the atmosphere, or environment, was our responsibility. Therefore we set the scene and refused to be dictated to or intimidated by the presiding atmosphere.

Sounds twee, but it is a reality.

The simplest way for us to understand this is to see that the leader is not a *thermometer*, which measures the temperature of the atmosphere set by followers, but a *thermostat*, which sets the temperature of the atmosphere that the followers come into.

We may understand this well enough when we are talking about actual temperature, measured in Celsius, but what about when we talk of a spiritual temperature, such as the level of faith or peace? What about when we talk of temperature in terms of excitement and expectancy?

Let's dig a little from our journey at Breathe City Church.

Over the last four years I can genuinely say I don't think we have had one Sunday that has not been totally explosive and where we haven't seen people make decisions to follow Jesus. So much so, that the thought of a Sunday going pear-shaped really isn't part of a BCCer's experience of church. This is possibly one of the reasons that people keep bringing their "not yet saved" friends – because they are confident that 1. A great experience of coming to church will be had and 2. They probably may just get saved!

The spiritual temperature of our Sundays doesn't happen by chance. It happens intentionally. And it happens by hard work and graft. We host a 9.00am, 11.00am, three 5.00pm's and then run ABC (new to church courses) at 6.30pm. The day is a full on day for the team, but what most don't realise is that it starts a lot earlier for the leaders, pastors, ministry directors and staff. At 5.45am there is a mass arrival of people at our Campus: City. At 6.00am, after copious amounts of coffee, we start to pray. Now I don't mean sit round in a circle and pass the prayer baton round and say "amen" after every prayer. I mean we absolutely storm heaven and call on God on behalf of BCCers and their guests. With shouts of praise and passionate yearning we intercede on behalf of the church and the city. We prophesy over the day and call people in from the north, south, east and west. Psalm 2:8 says,

"Ask of me and I will make the nations your inheritance."

So we ask.

James 5:16 tells us that the prayer of a righteous man is effective, right? Do we genuinely believe this scripture? We do and that is why we place such importance on this explosive start to the day. We come together and speak life into our day and set the temperature of faith to boiling point. We intentionally train our leaders to get to grips with the reality of this and everyone knows that the time of prayer isn't for the faint hearted. I personally lead that time together and I refuse to let any moment subside or become melancholic.

The atmosphere that our people walk into is explosive. Yes, we work on the ambience of our facilities and yes, we are strategic in the music we play and concerned about details such as the lighting levels and the haze and the visuals carrying faith-filled scriptures and wording. However, I personally believe that the buzz created in our gathering is a supernatural buzz that is intentionally initiated by this hot house of prayer.

3.2 | Social Media and BBM

Building church in the 21st Century is obviously very different from previous centuries. I'm told that life is far more hectic and people are more precious about their time, as many are working longer hours and travelling takes up huge parts of our day also. I'm told that another negative is that we are building church in a far more secular society and people are further from the Church and an understanding of God than ever before. I'm told there are several other negative connotations to building church in this Google Generation.

However, I personally believe that the positives far outweigh the negatives and it is actually easier for us to build church in this generation than ever before, due to the resources we have available to us to engage with people. In this generation of communication and technological advances we have so much at our fingertips to make the most of.

Many churches have begun to understand the power of the World Wide Web and many have websites. On this, please: the web is a shop window, so please ensure websites are just that and not the back room closet where the dirty laundry is stashed. Some websites are simply shocking. Listen, many will not come on a Sunday morning as the first thing they will do is to look at the website. If the website is "super spiritual", really badly designed or simply naff – people won't come to visit you on Sunday morning. Others have begun to engage with Facebook and have created groups so that discussions and information can be given out — which is really good. We knew that, in such a fast paced world, we had to find a platform that was also fast paced. With regard to social media there is huge power to be harnessed if used smartly.

We use Twitter.

And we use Twitter very, very intentionally.

There is a public aspect and a private aspect. Let me share both with you.

As soon as people come into the life of BCC we really encourage them to get on Twitter. We talk about it from the pulpit, we write about it, we use it incessantly and it is really part of our operation. We use it in our preaching in a very interactive way and we constantly pass 140 characters worth of headlines regarding what is happening at every layer of our organisation. Every ministry has an account, every pastor, every leader and every staff member. The reality is, there is a tsunami of news being broadcast on Twitter from Breathe City Church. After every meeting praise reports and "Twitpics" are beamed across the social media platform and quite literally thousands, tens of thousands of people read them. Furthermore, as BCCers see other BCCers' tweets, we have now intentionally developed the trend to RT others. For those not familiar with Twitter, an RT (Re-Tweet) is to copy someone else's tweet and send it to your followers.

At a recent day conference we hosted, the geeks amongst us worked out that tweets from that day would have had the cumulative audience of nearly 15,000 people. Now that is some audience which is receiving information, comments, pictures and good reports about what is happening at BCC. We have to understand the power of social media in this generation. It is now social media that keeps people up to date with world affairs, not the 6 o'clock news. It is tweets that report on wars in the Middle East, not the newspapers. And it is social media that can carry the message of what Jesus is building!

The private aspect of this is BBM.

BlackBerry Messenger for those who are really confused.

We have done something that, I believe, is very exciting and very, very intentional.

A number of years ago, I made the decision that we could access what people in the corporate world were discovering. We are told that BBM had a huge part in creating the momentum of the chaotic scenes we saw in the summer of 2011, that are now infamously called the London Riots. BBM is also causing a revolution in Stoke-on-Trent and the building of a great church.

We obviously aren't able to enforce this issue, but it has been caught hold of and, if not caught hold of, taught to our leaders and pastors. Nearly everyone has a BlackBerry. Some also have an iPhone.

The BlackBerry, with the technology of RIM, has what is known as BBM. BlackBerry Messenger. BBM is basically group texting that everyone in the group can engage with. It's a tech version of a chat room. What this facilitates is that, as an organisation, we are online and in constant communication with each other. Whatever is happening, wherever we are, we are always in sync with each other. It would be my understanding that our efficiency levels have increased by 40% due to this constant, in-touch communication. As a large organisation with nearly 90 ministries operating across 10 sites in our city, we can still move at the drop of a hat and spin on a sixpence.

Here's an example tied to Twitter to demonstrate our intentionality. Let's say our Comms Team (Communications) produced a short film highlighting something amazing that Jesus is doing. Say it was one of our City Transformations videos which tell the story of BCCers and how God has changed their life. A lack of intention is that I put a tweet up saying how good the video is. A better way would be to direct people to watch the video. An even better way is to put up a link to the video. This is where most stop.

They hope that people will watch the video.

However, intentionality and the power of BBM gives the hope of people watching the video a little more chance. Once the link and message to watch the video is put on Twitter, instantly a message across the infrastructure of the church is sent to all pastors, leaders, staff and ministry directors to also promote the tweet. Within seconds the tweet has been RT'd many, many times over and tens of thousands of people will now be reading that same tweet. It therefore doesn't surprise us, when looking at the statistics of the video uploads, to see the volume of people who have watched that message of a changed life. Quite literally thousands of people have watched that video of Jesus changing someone's life.

We set up a food bank in our city, in a one week turn around when, at the drop of a hat we communicated the idea to our pastors, leaders, ministry directors and staff. £60,000 worth of food was collected and stocked, all because of the constant communication on BBM. There are many more stories, but this gives you a taste of intentionality using technology.

3.3 | Catalysts For Growth

I believe that all healthy things grow! The reality is that it is the responsibility of the leader to ensure that health is a priority. In my last book I wrote about Health being one of the cultural pillars of our church. I would also be as bold to say that one evidence of a healthy church is the growth of that church. There are other things that reveal the evidence of a healthy church, but we must never hide away from looking for growth.

In the story of Jonathan and his armour bearer, we read that the first word that Jonathan uttered was "Come". The Hebrew word for "come" is *nagash* (naw gash) which means "to be (at a place) for a purpose". In Greek "come" is translated *deuro* which can be described as an imperative and means "hither" (it carries both an intensity and is time related).

For Jonathan there is an eagerness to be in a place that he knows carries a purpose.

When looking at the church being built and when I compare the observations of Exodus 18:21 and Deuteronomy 1:15, I see that growth primarily has to do with the mandate or anointing that God has ordained. We often pursue church growth as unlimited and many a church leader is frustrated because they feel that their church should be bigger. But what happens if God has ordained that I have the capacity, ability and anointing to lead a certain number of people? What is that number?

I don't know ... these are simply questions that I have.

What I do know is that I don't want to waste time waiting to see if the church will grow. I believe that Jesus is building His Church and healthy things grow. Therefore, like Jonathan, there is an urgency to see the church grow numerically, financially, in our effectiveness of ministry to our city and in our influence.

And it is obviously time related, since we never know how much time we have. We do have today, however.

Therefore we are very intentional in seeing this healthy church demonstrate healthy fruit by the evidence of growth. Here are three intentional ways of focusing on and harnessing growth.

The Core

Throughout Scripture we are given the example of working with what we have, not what we have not – whether it is observing Jesus and His disciples, David and his mighty men or the parable of the talents.

It is absolutely essential to invest in those who carry the vision and cast the vision. We began by putting on events to gather a crowd. We invited bands such as Planetshakers and we looked to gather a number of people. What dawned on me was that gathering a crowd was not the same as building a church and the same volume of finance that brought great bands in could be used to build our leaders. We decided to scrap the "gather a crowd" model and started inviting the nations' best leaders to spend time with our core people.

What happened was exactly what we wanted to happen.

Bigger churches exist because of bigger people. As the leaders were equipped and empowered to follow, their leadership increased and therefore they started leading more people and a swell of followship occurred and the church started to, and continues to, grow. Intentionally invest in your core.

Create the Catalysts

I have been in full time ministry since 1996 and have seen a vast amount of church activity. For a number of years I genuinely thought that catalysts were occasional and miraculous; something would happen that triggered a small aspect of momentum. These catalysts in my thinking became almost like nuggets of gold that I constantly looked out for. Until one day, it dawned on me that catalysts can be created. In 1 Kings 18 we see Elijah create a catalyst. Yes, it was supernatural and yes, God intervened, but Elijah was simply creating space for God to move. We have to create space for God to move. My father always used to say, "Give God an opportunity to perform a miracle." This is the kind of catalyst that I am talking about creating!

Remember in Part One where I wrote about "I AM JOSEPH – the journey of becoming"? It was about the lessons we can learn from Joseph's life in walking towards the fulfilment of all that God has in store. It is based on a series I'm preaching on, but as well as being a series it is also a catalyst that has been created. The way that we have advertised the series, its marketing and its promotion, has generated so much interest that it has started a momentum of growth.

People have captured the seed of thought regarding their destiny and the fulfilment of why we are on planet earth: to bring "not yet saved" friends who need to hear a message of faith, hope and love so that they do get saved. People are responding and rekindling past dreams and new ministries are starting. It is a catalyst. God is moving, but we have to move first to see God move!

Conversion Rate

The final intentional aspect that helps stimulate growth is the speed at which we operate. BCC is a fast moving church. It has a huge volume of momentum and that momentum has to be managed and maintained. This is done by our ability and capacity to move fast, as previously stated, but also includes the speed at which we make decisions. We have to convert our thoughts and ideas into actions.

In general, we English are very conservative. We like to mull things over and take our time so as not to make mistakes. The reality is, we take ourselves too seriously. Really, if it doesn't work, it is only our ego that takes a bashing. We have intentionally built into the life of our church – a "let's give it a whirl", "what have we got to lose" mindset. We are not flippant about our decision making, but we most definitely don't regard ourselves to be that important. We have specifically taught our people that, as a church, we want to be God's guinea pig. He can experiment with us! This creates such momentum that people get pulled along with the tidal wave of opportunities that come our way because we are always on the lookout to see what we can do, what God is doing and what could happen if someone did something. Thus, growth is generated as more and more ministries are established and more and more people touched.

3.4 | Doing Life and Being Church

Followship is very different from attendance.

The reality of church life is that unless followship is established then a few follow and the crowd attends. That is the main contributing reason why many churches and church leaders constantly struggle to raise volunteers. It is the same reason why many a leader capitulates to the 80:20 rule that says 80% of the work is done by 20% of the people. The foundational psychology of this scenario is that it is based upon an institutional framework of understanding regarding what it is to be church. This framework of understanding has to be dealt with if followship is to be established.

There has to come a move from institutional to relational. There has to come a paradigm shift from "I go to church" to "I am church".

Remember "caught and taught"? Yes, some will catch this, but the majority will need to be taught.

This can be done intentionally.

Not only did this process occur intentionally for us, but it was done very obviously. Remember the part of Scripture where Paul says, "NOTICE WHAT LARGE LETTERS I USE AS I WRITE THESE CLOSING WORDS IN MY OWN HANDWRITING" (Galatians 6:11). Well, this process occurred in that obvious fashion.

I preached about us "being" the church and we broadcast this message through the whole life of our church, including visuals and graphics, avatars and leaflet distribution. We created a hash tag for Twitter trending and even included it in our Visual Standards Policy (our branding guide). The message was simply:

#IAMBCC

Acts 17:28 says that, *"For in Him we live and move and exist..."*

It is in Jesus Christ that we have our identity.

We are the body of Christ. When we think about that physically, Jesus would look really disturbing if His head, which it is, was perfect, but His body was weak and disfigured.

When Paul writes to the church in Ephesus, he gives a real insight into who we are as the Church. The body of Christ is called to BE!

Ephesians 1:23 says that, *"The church is His body; it is made full and complete by Christ, who fills all things everywhere with himself."*

Therefore we don't go to church, we are the church and He is mobilising us as His body to be the Church and fill all things everywhere.

Ephesians chapter 2 gives us insight into how we should "be the church".

The first observation is that we should **Turn Up!** I don't merely mean turn up as in "arrive", I mean TURN UP! Be here fully – as in: when I'm here, I'm here! As in: if I am the church, then I must TURN UP on Monday morning as much as I do on Sunday morning. Ephesians 2:1-10 tells the reader that they are alive in Christ Jesus. It clearly tells us that we are saved and that salvation is not because of us but because of Jesus. Paul tells the reader, in essence (my paraphrase) to "cheer up, believe in yourself, you're awesome – you are God's masterpiece. You were once dead and now you are alive."

Axioms like "today will never happen again" began to impress upon the church about living full lives and making the most of every opportunity. We began to understand that we all get 24 hours in a day and we need to turn up fully, because we are the body of Christ, the Church, and He fills all things everywhere with Himself. We're bringing our A-game every day.

When you see the enthusiasm and excitement in BCCers' daily activity, it is evident that this revelation has captured their hearts.

Ephesians 2:11-13 gives us further insight into "being the church". Paul begins to angle his writing to the church in Ephesus to stir them to **Stand Up**. In reading his words one can imagine the passion that he is intentionally putting into his writing to stir the church to rise and Stand Up, to believe in itself. He writes saying that they shouldn't forget that, as Gentiles, they were once outsiders and called "uncircumcised heathens", and how in those days they were living apart from Christ. Now, however, they have been united with Christ and brought near. It's a rousing few sentences that are designed to stir the Church to stand up and be counted; to understand the journey that they have been on; to realise they have moved from being outside to now being united with Christ.

What this did with BCCers was to allow them the permission, in the best sense of the word, to be proud of who they were. They were no longer "outsiders", "losers" or "rejects", they were "united with Christ" – you know, the One who conquered death! BCCers started to Stand Up in their work places. They started to Stand Up in their communities. Together they started to Stand Up and be salt and light ... They started following!

In being the church, the body of Christ, we next have to **Speak Up** and speak up in unity or one voice. Ephesians 2:14-15 reveals again that Christ brought peace and ended the dominion of the Law with its commands and regulations. Christ brings peace and He brings unity. We began to grasp that as His body, or in "being the church", we had to model His behaviour. Understanding that the tongue has the power of life and death (Proverbs 18:21) together we could Speak Up for that which Jesus does in bringing peace and unity. The message from the church has to be clear and in one voice: we speak for peace and unity; we champion our city and don't criticise it. Again, we built an axiom around this and we call our city the "centre of the universe" (which it is!).

Finally we look at Ephesians 2:16-22 and we conclude that we should **Live Up**! This has to do with the idea that we are being built together, therefore we are dependent upon one another. One person's success is dependent on another's. We are being built together, so the most sensible thing is to Live Up – not to plateau or regress, but encourage one another and help one another. Doing life together and being the church is such a wonderful release of understanding.

This is something we do. It is who we are. The relationships are intertwined.

This didn't simply happen. It happened intentionally and obviously.

3.5 | Creating a Whinge Free Environment

Followship is a sensational thought, but the reality is that it must have some very obvious opposition, otherwise it would not be so rare. One of the contributing forces that oppose great followship is the "Whinge".

We all know what it is, but how do we combat it? For a long time I thought that the whinge was something that, at best, could be contained. But as I began to discover intentionality, I also began to discover that the whinge could be eradicated by creating a "whinge free" environment.

Looking at the journey of the spies who entered into the Promised Land in Deuteronomy 1:19-25 and Numbers 13:26-33 we can see that the "whinge" always gets its way, even if there are positive, visionary leaders. I decided that I would no longer live in the same house as the whinge, so I evicted it!

This is how we intentionally evicted the whinge and established a whinge free environment where followship flourishes.

Paul, writing to the church in Philippi, said something that caught my attention. Recognising Paul's intentionality, I instantly thought, "I wonder why he wrote that?"

In Philippians 2:14 he instructs, *"Do everything without complaining..."*

I mean, look at the lack of room he is giving the whinge. He clearly gives not one inch when he uses the word "everything".

As in EVERYTHING!!!

He highlights the result of this way of conduct slightly further on (v15) when he encourages them then to *"shine like stars"*.

That was the intentionality right there. The whinge doesn't shine!

It's a choice we began presenting the church with: "Be a winner or a whinger!" Evidently no one wanted to be labelled a whinger, so even the whingers chose to pursue what it was to be a winner.

Here were the "helpers" we gave to people to help them get on and keep on the winner's path! As this became a reality, the whinge was evicted!

Rejoice

Paul tells the Philippians to Rejoice! (2:18) We have to look at the context of Paul's writing. He has confronted the church in Philippi with the no nonsense "do everything without complaining" and then gives them some further instruction. The intentional aspect is that he then issues a complete full stop, end of the conversation, "talk to the hand" statement by saying, "Yes, you should rejoice, and I will share with your joy!" In other words, "that's the end of the matter, now rejoice and I will be checking. I will share in your joy because that is how you are to receive my instruction." See why I like Paul so much?

Caleb and Joshua were rejoicing in where they had just been – it was a great place – but the whinge drowned them out. Paul doesn't allow the whinge any room. Refuse to engage with the whinge like Paul did.

The other thing that Paul told the church in Philippi, which was very clever and I believe to be very intentional, before confronting the whinge, was that God was working in them (2:13). In other words, humility is key here. The whinge stems from self. Humility is the counter balance to self-rising. It is said that Humility is God's plan A and His plan B is Humiliation. The whinge doesn't want to be found out and humiliated, so an embrace of humility begins to quieten down the whinge. The great thing about Caleb and Joshua is that we can see humility in their words. They recognised God at work and knew that God would act on their behalf. The whinge from the other ten spies was purely selfish, moaning about how they felt as small as grasshoppers and how they couldn't do it.

A few more things can be pulled from Caleb and Joshua. Only Caleb and Joshua entered the Promised Land. Deuteronomy 1 shows that because the people weren't grateful that, (i) God spoke and (ii) had great plans for them, that they would never enter the promise. The whinge is spoilt and ungrateful. As a church we began to publicly celebrate what God had given us: the buildings, the people, the privilege, the opportunities. We flooded the conversation of the church with grateful gestures.

Be intentional again with this. We have so much to thank God for. With open eyes we can see that God has blessed us and with an open mouth we can tell others, who in turn will tell others. Followship thrives on a good report!

Caleb and Joshua chose to think and see the best. Paul talks to the church in Philippi about holding on to their faith. The amazing thing is that when we choose to think and see the best in every situation we step into faith.

We believe that God is doing something.

We believe that the best is yet to come.

We believe that the tide always turns and we believe that victory can be had.

We believe that things will get better and we believe that we are making progress.

The Bible clearly says that it is impossible to please God without faith (Hebrews 11:6) and as we see and think the best, this is exactly what happens. The whinge is evicted and faith rises. As faith rises, God smiles upon us. People start to see the evidence of God's smile and are drawn to it. Followship begins to be firmly established!

3.6 | Team Driven

In order to establish great followship, intentional thinking must again be applied. The very root or essence of the new word we've created implies not one shred of individualism. By its very fragrance, the word followship implies a corporate dimension. There is a togetherness, a glue, a oneness that is so attached to the word.

Therefore, in light of what we learnt from the armour bearer and what is caught or taught to the 600 men and the Hebrews in the caves, an example is very much needed. In the light of leadership being visual, a very obvious example of followship has to be modelled.

That is why team is so important.

If there is any thought that the number one leader can individually create followship, then we have missed the understanding and concept of this new word.

Due to this, establishing an excellent team that thoroughly understands "team" and can very much model followship to the rest of the church needs to be established, and it needs to be done in a very public way. Therefore, the private conversations must also be very intentional and my experience and thus suggestion would be to be as deliberate in selecting and building team as possible. Then the public expression will be seen and applauded as a great team giving a great example of followship, thus creating a swell of great followship.

Paul, when writing to the Church in Rome, again drops in some comments that I think are helpful before we address this issue. In Romans 12 Paul gives so many nuggets of revelation regarding doing life with each other that, if applied to team and the building of team, are even more exaggerated.

Briefly, he talks of not being conformed to the patterns of this world, having a new mindset, to think soberly, to understand there are many parts of one body, diverse in gifting, to love each other and not merely pretend, to delight in honouring one another, to never be lazy, to be enthusiastic, to be of hope, to understand patience, to bless those who give you a hard time, to live in harmony, keep it real, that two wrongs never make a right and to live in peace. The chapter concludes with a victorious "conquer evil by doing good"!

If we grasped this chapter alone we would develop world class teams.

Get things clear in private and it will be seen in public.

Know your Leader's Heart. It is essential that the leader clearly speaks that which is on their heart. This really has to be done consistently because the team really needs to know who they are following and how they tick.

Know your Leader's Vision. Again, totally essential. Once a team "gets" the leader, they are able to understand in a much clearer way the vision that the leader is carrying.

Leaders need to be vulnerable and transparent here so that who they really are and what they really see is seen, caught or taught.

Know your Leader's Strengths (and weaknesses). Evidently the leader isn't perfect yet. Evidently they carry some strengths. If a team member has anything to learn it is that no other seat feels like the number one seat. Teams need to do their utmost to help the leader. A great way to do this is realise that they aren't superman and then use their gifts, as a team, to ensure that the team is strong and the leader is secure!

Know your Place. A team will never be efficient if people don't know their place. The reality is that a team member's place will often change. The issue is to not find solace in knowing what you do, but in who you are. You are on the team not because of what you do, but because of who you are. You are the gift not your skill set! This is important. People need to see secure leaders for them to feel secure, otherwise they won't follow.

Know your Team. Again, knowing each other is just as important as knowing the leader. The relationships need to work not just with the leader, but also across the team. Otherwise, when the leader is missing there will be no connection.

Know your Requirements. Get your brief and fulfil it. The team is absolutely dependent on the team. "As strong as the weakest link" is still a phrase that is applicable. Therefore, get clear on your responsibilities and then deliver and deliver strong. What the 600 soldiers and Hebrews hiding in the caves saw was Jonathan and his armour bearer working so wonderfully together that it looked choreographed! They were given a physical representation of harmony.

Know you're Called. Again, this is really important. A person who is a great team player knows that they have been called. They weren't merely the last in line and so had to be picked. They are as called to the team. They are there to serve the leader, but they are called as an individual. Whilst the leader requires them, that mandate is upon them!

Know you're Appreciated. Please listen. Mistakes may occur, the ball may be dropped, but you are still appreciated. Hopefully, the leader is learning how to thank you and learning to thank you really well, but have grace. Understand that they are on a journey too and may not always get to say it, but they do appreciate you!

Know your Potential. Finally, the individual and the team need to have the revelation that they are not the finished deal. There is so much more ahead. Followers need to see that you are learning and developing continuously. That helps with followship. Being vulnerable and transparent is a good thing. Therefore realise you aren't perfect and at the same time allow the potential of the future, that which lies ahead, to excite you. People follow people who are going somewhere.

As the team begins to drive forward it creates enough space for the people to see the improvement, thus a model is created for people to follow ... and they do! Followship is being established.

3.7 | Rocks & Crocks

The reality is that even when followship is established, the journey of leadership is not complete. One of the harsh realities of leadership is that nothing lasts forever. One of the most devastating things a church leader can do is think that things are sorted.

Nothing lasts forever.

Bill Hybels says, "Nothing rocks forever."

One of the best ways for a leader to stay in front is to develop the skill of evaluation and learn that facts are our friends. These are two key elements that have to be intentionally built into the life and systems of the church to force a leader's hand. I say "force a leader's hand" because leaders, generally speaking, are visionaries and are more inclined to see forward than look at the present or the past.

However, for followship to continue and maintain momentum, a leader has to stay in front and keep the church moving forward. This is done by ensuring the "whole" is continuously evaluated in an honest fashion and then addressed. Followship can help in this process, but followers must see that the leadership is secure and strong enough to lead this process.

I'll say it again: the skill of evaluation and learning that facts are our friends are two key elements that must be intentionally built into the life and systems of the church.

One way that we have successfully (and at first painfully) done this is to develop what is commonly known as The Bell Test. The

Bell Test is a great way to evaluate every area of church life and ask, "What Rocks and What Crocks?"

Remembering that facts are our friends when carrying out this evaluation exercise not only lets the leaders know about the progress of the church, but also facilitates healthy and holistic followship because, if done properly, it stops things from heading south and keeps things advancing. When things are moving forward, it's a lot easier to follow.

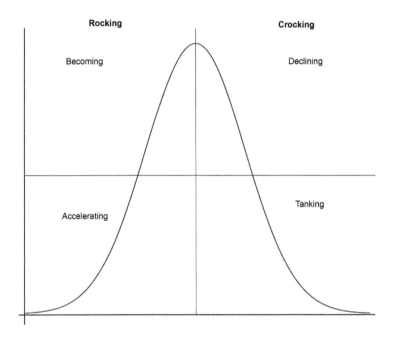

As you can see in the diagram opposite, the shape of the bell moves through four quadrants: Accelerating, Becoming, Declining and Tanking. The aim of the exercise is honest evaluation.

Pick any given area in the life of the church e.g. Youth Ministry and ask yourself, "Is the Youth Ministry Accelerating, Becoming, Declining or Tanking?"

So for us, the conversation could go something like,

A. So, let's take City Youth ... How is it going?

B. Well, from my perspective it's doing really well. New young people are getting saved every week. It's growing and still keeping to budget.

A. Great. Which quadrant would you put it in?

B. Oh, definitely Becoming.

A. OK, great. Now where on the line is it in the quadrant?

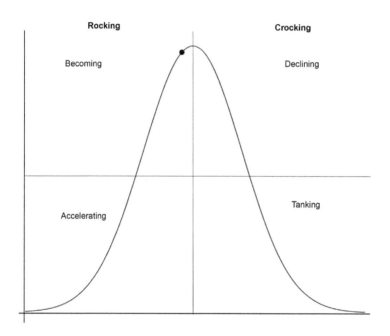

B. Well, I don't know really ... it's all good, but I've seen some tensions within the team and maybe that's birthed out of familiarity.

A. Interesting. Anything else?

B. I mean, if we're really digging down on this, we're slightly behind on our annual targets, the presence of God hasn't been as evident the last couple of Friday nights and maybe City Youth hasn't been supporting the other ministries of the church as much as it should.

A. OK, so actually it's right at the top of the curve?

B. Yeah, I guess you could say that we're cruising and now maybe plateauing...

A. So we know what comes next unless we intervene?

B. Wow ... Decline?

A. Yep! So what do we do now to keep the thing Becoming rather than Declining?

B. Hey Pastor, I thought we were doing well, but ... yeah, actually we've levelled out and if I don't address the relational tensions, maybe relocating a few people, and keep the spiritual atmosphere hot, then we'll start Declining.

A. Brilliant. Let's get working on that issue for the next few months and let's keep pushing this baby forward!

B. Absolutely!

This is one scenario and one conversation that could be had using The Bell Test in evaluating any given area of church life. It also draws out the reality that facts are our friends and we don't have to paint a rosy picture all the time. From a place of honesty, effective strategy can be birthed.

What happened in the hypothetical conversation above is that initial observations, which were heavily biased, were simply given a reality check. The City Youth Lead could begin to see things the way they really were in the context of The Bell Test. This resulted in an action plan being formulated to deal with the pressing issues and thus allow the Youth Ministry to keep Becoming rather than Declining.

One other very intentional tool we use here at BCC alongside The Bell Test is the 3Rs. When discussing areas in the life of the church we have to recognise that it is pretty much all built on people, living stones. The 3Rs are simply an effective way of helping people engage in a more effective way and not become bottlenecks and obstacles to progress.

The three Rs are:

Re-train: Where a person simply needs advanced training to help them become more efficient and effective in their functionality.

Relocate: Where it is now evident that this person would be better suited to a different area of church life thus causing that person to thrive and not get frustrated (hence the comment about "relocation" in the above scenario).

Retire: This is where it is pretty evident that taking some time out from functioning would be, let's say, "beneficial" to all parties concerned.

Nothing rocks forever and it is the primary responsibility of the senior leader to engage with and stimulate the evaluation of the church and learn that facts are our friends. When this gets into the systems and life of the church, then the whole church becomes accountable to the future. Leaders can advance and see vision fulfilled. Followers get to see that they are doing a great job and find fulfilment in their roles and become bigger people as a result.

3.8 | Three Chairs

In regard to establishing followship, much of what has been discussed so far has been mostly to do with mindset – challenging and shifting paradigms in order to see things from a different perspective and thus operate in a different fashion in order to see more advantageous results: more people coming into the life of the church, more communities reached with the sensational and life-giving message of Jesus and more people mobilised in fulfilling the vision of the church.

The issue of followship is not merely to do with mindset. It also goes with culture, although we know culture to be a huge influence in facilitating great followship. There is a hard wiring to this issue. There are practical and systematic ways, methods and strategies that can be used to enhance followship becoming a reality.

I've come to know one given method as "The Three Chairs Rule".

The Three Chairs Rule dramatically enhanced the efficiency of our infrastructure and it came out of an experiment in one of our staff meetings. Now, as an off-shoot, the staff meetings of our organisation are all about productivity and delivery. I would expect my staff to be doing their devotions and musings in their own time. They aren't paid to develop their spiritual disciplines, they are paid to fulfil a role in the life of the church. I don't pay the rest of the congregation to fulfil their spiritual disciplines, but I still expect them to read their Bible, pray and spend time with the Father before they start their day. It's the same with our staff.

Back to the discussion.

In a staff meeting we began to unpack the fact that my proximity to people was getting less and less as we began to grow. It also became apparent that even "face time" with those who were beyond three tiers (or "chairs") away from me in the organisational structure was also diminishing. This was initially alarming to me and most concerned me when my Ministries Executive and Young Adults Stream Pastor appointed the City Youth Lead with me having hardly any input and only seeing the appointee for five minutes at an event that we held. It dawned on me that my ability to delegate was critical, but I had to ensure that I didn't defer instead. True delegation empowers and resources, feeds back and is held accountable. To defer means that the leader let's go and has then lost sight and lost hold on certain activities or areas, which are then free to wander where they like. So in order to help our delegation and ensure that "touch" was always in place across the organisation, we established "The Three Chair Rule".

What is The Three Chair Rule?

Effectively, within the organisation, we ensure that the three chairs behind are always filled. Or, put another way, that the three positions of responsibility that follow a leader are always filled by competent people. (See the segment of our Organisational Structure opposite as I begin to explain this further).

As the Senior Pastor I am in CHAIR 1. Therefore, I must ensure that CHAIR 2 and CHAIR 3 are filled. I have done this with our Primary Leadership Team in CHAIR 2 and (in this scenario) Ministries Executive in CHAIR 3.

My three chairs are filled. This means that I have placed competent people in positions of responsibility. I really mustn't interfere beyond the third chair if I am to help and not hinder the establishment of followship. I have delegated and am empowering the three chairs that I am to touch. Beyond that, my input or involvement must come only by invite or critical intervention, if required.

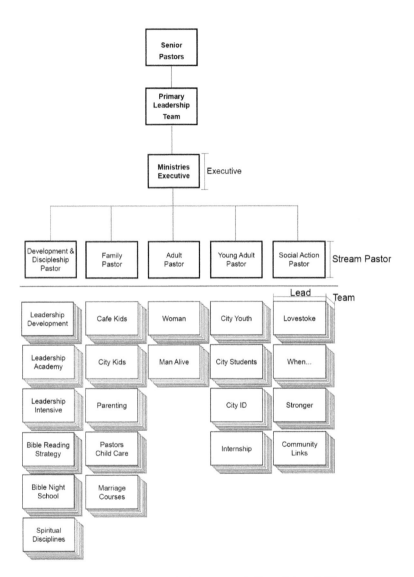

(One of five sectors from BCC organisational structure, used with permission of BCC)

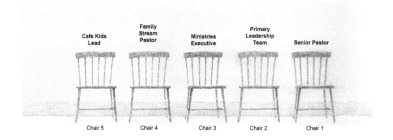

Let us move this on further. The Primary Leadership Team must now ensure that three chairs are also filled. The Primary Leadership Team is now classed as CHAIR 1. The Ministries Executive (appointed by me as Senior Pastor) is already established as CHAIR 2. Now CHAIR 3 has to be established. CHAIR 1 and CHAIR 2 have to work to set CHAIR 3 in place. In this example CHAIR 3 is Family Stream Pastor.

Let's continue to follow this through. Now the Ministries Executive is in CHAIR 1 and we have already established CHAIR 2 as the Family Stream Pastor. The appointment of CHAIR 3 is now beyond my daily and obvious reach and the Primary Leadership Team should be allowing the Ministries Executive and the Family Stream Pastor space to select and establish CHAIR 3, which in this case is the Café Kids Lead.

This "Rule" continues through the life of the Organisational Structure.

Three things have become very apparent to us here at Breathe City Church following The Three Chair Rule.

Firstly, it empowers delegation and releases the armour bearers to not merely follow, but also to have the authority and responsibility to lead without being imposed upon. This is critical for followship to be established because it allows people to thrive, which is so important in church life. If a person feels the weight of constantly following when they have the gift of leadership, they tend to become frustrated, even exasperated. The Three Chair Rule gives people space to thrive.

Secondly, it clearly maps out responsibilities and boundaries for operation. The Three Chair Rule eradicates "interfering". Anything beyond three chairs is being taken care of, and this actually empowers leaders to look forwards not backwards, look up and not down, look further and not immediate. Primary Leadership Team meetings now are purely focused on vision, moving forward, and leadership contextual conversations. Management and "now issues" are taken care of by Executives, and the day to day issues of life are being diligently handled by Directors and Pastors (who are so fantastic at doing this! I thank God for our Directors and Pastors every day – they are amazing people!)

The third thing that is very evident, which again came out of that staff meeting, is that we perceive that every chair represents approximately 200 people. When only CHAIR 1 was filled there was no way that BCC was going to break 200. When CHAIR 2 was correctly filled we grew to 400. When CHAIR 3 was correctly filled we grew to 600. We observed that across the organisation we generally have five chairs filled and we are around 1,000 in number. This also works within ministries. Under our Family Stream Pastor, within our Cafe: Kids ministry, we have in excess of 1,000 in attendance and, interestingly, five chairs are very much established.

The Three Chair Rule works! We now literally line up chairs, like on a train, and work through the chairs being filled. Where chairs are not filled we clearly see the organisation is suffering. Where the chairs are filled, we clearly see that the organisation is thriving.

This is a practical and systematic approach to establishing great followship. The leader has to fill three chairs first and be very intentional in doing so, exampling it to CHAIR 2 and CHAIR 3, and then be committed to delegating and not interfering thereafter.

Part Four: Practical Working Examples

4.1 | The Art of Delegation

By now we have understood that a crowd of attendees will not translate into great followship. The essence of followship is that it is a corporate understanding of people who are excellent at following. This means that they have to have something, or someone, to follow. As seen in the story of Jonathan, a leader is best at leading armour bearers or people who are close to them.

In other terms that we have used, the leader will lead the Vision Casters and Carriers best. The Vision Casters and Carriers, or armour bearers, will lead the people and this is where the swell of followship is created as the people follow the Vision Castors and Carriers.

The leadership, therefore, must fully utilise the followship. As already stated, followship is not merely attendees, followship is great people who know how to follow.

Looking at the examples of Jesus in the His training of the disciples we see that a great follower is a person who is able to walk in the leader's footsteps, carry the burden of the vision and take on roles and activities that are distributed.

Take Jesus at the feeding of the five thousand in Luke 9.

In verse 14 Jesus said to His disciples, *"Tell them to sit down in groups of fifty each."*

Why is this important? Well, it's very important because Jesus is modelling something that we later see re-emerge in Acts 6. Have a look at what Jesus does.

He doesn't merely give an instruction, He delegates. And He delegates well.

Most leaders in this position would have addressed the crowd themselves, asking people to break into fifties and then got the disciples to distribute the food. That is not what Jesus does. He empowers the disciples with both the strategy and the provision, but it is very clear who does the ministry.

The art of delegation is really important if we are to empower and stimulate great followship.

Delegation is not being a task master. It is not giving out the jobs that the leader hasn't got time for. It is all about empowerment and it is all about building a platform for others and allowing them to thrive.

The easiest way to help leaders grasp the art of delegation is what I've come to term the "Why, What and How Principle".

The Why, What and How Principle is something we use at BCC to help train all our leaders and it works exceptionally well because it shows the boundaries of responsibility and authority.

The reason why many leaders get frustrated and the "control freak" rises up and pronounces those demonic words, "It's easier to just do it myself," is not because a follower isn't doing something right. The reason the leader is frustrated with the follower is because the leader is doing it wrong. There is a process to delegation. It is an art.

The first place to start is to understand that the leader is a control freak. They have a vision and they, before God, are responsible for seeing the fulfilment of what they envision. Therefore, the leader needs to realise that they shouldn't let go of their responsibility straight away. There is a process.

Stage one is that the leader must retain the WHY and the WHAT. The first stage is to even retain the HOW. The leader should explain very carefully HOW they want something to be done. Too many times leaders ask a person to do something (which is the WHAT), but don't clearly explain HOW it needs to be done.

Stage one is complete when the follower has successfully demonstrated that they understand HOW and then do the task or role exactly as shown. The process of delegation must not go any further until this stage is successful. The mistake that is made is that the leader jumps stages before How is working successfully.

Stage two is only for the follower who has successfully mastered the HOW. Only when the follower has competently demonstrated that they know HOW something is to be done, and the leader is satisfied that this is so, can the leader then continue with the process. What occurs now is that the leader retains the WHY, clearly explains the WHAT, but should now have fully released the HOW. In fact, the leader should be secure enough at this stage to not concern himself with the HOW. The leader should trust that the follower can do the HOW, even do it better than the leader first expressed.

Problems arise when the leader doesn't follow this principle.

The leader should sit with the follower and discuss the WHAT at length. The leader can hint at the WHY, but must retain the WHY. As the leader explains WHAT they want doing the follower who is successfully holding the HOW will begin to grasp the WHAT. As they take hold of the WHAT they will in turn be training someone with the HOW. As this stage takes shape and progresses, what occurs is that the follower now takes full reign of the WHAT and the leader lets go and only retains the WHY. The follower can now also release the HOW to a second follower and delegation is really occurring. Followship is being empowered.

The leader should never jump stages forward or jump stages backward. The HOW is now completely released. The leader should be totally trusting and empowering the followers to be responsible for this.

The leader should then be focused and fixed on handling the WHY. When the follower holding the WHAT is proving themselves successful and competent, and the leader is satisfied, the leader can then consider whether they would prefer for that follower to release the WHAT and begin to help the leader with the WHY.

The leader never lets go of the WHY.

A practical example. Train someone in HOW you want people to be *welcomed*. Once achieved, train that same person in WHAT (the WHAT in this case is what the leader wants to happen: people receive a great *welcome*). As that person grasps the WHAT, they will train others in HOW to do it and their training will be better that the original HOW because of their gifting and personal development. When the WHAT is established, the leader can consider the person to help with the WHY (the WHY in any scenario is the reason or purpose of any given activity.)

The Why, What and How principle works.

4.2 | Understanding Natural, Zonal and Positional Leadership

The reason why great followership is not established is simply because of a poor understanding of leadership. Followers get very frustrated at being pigeonholed or even put in the wrong hole. Volunteers stop volunteering as a sense of fulfilment and achievement is not experienced. Leaders get frustrated with followers when the follower does not fulfil that which is released to them or they fail to deliver in a certain area.

This book is designed to give insight into how, intentionally, a leader is to facilitate and create great followership.

One of the great insights we have made is the key understanding of *natural, zonal* and *positional leadership*. Once understood, this insight gives the leader the foresight to be very intentional with regard to working with people's strengths. It also eradicates the frustrations of why people fail to deliver or live up to their perceived potential.

The story of Jesus and His conversation with the Roman Officer lends a hand in our understanding. The centurion says something that is very revealing about leadership in Luke 7:6-8:

"'Lord, don't trouble yourself by coming to my home, for I am not worthy of such an honour. I am not even worthy to come and meet you. Just say the word from where you are, and my servant will be healed. I know this because I am under the authority of my superior officers, and I have authority over my soldiers. I only need to say 'Go,' and they go, or 'Come,' and they come. And if I say to my slaves, 'Do this,' they do it.'"

What we have here is recognition of authority, responsibility, delegated authority and delegated responsibility.

The Roman Officer is clear that Jesus has authority. He is also clear that he has authority in two areas of his own life and explains the difference. He has authority in his work situation because he is under authority. The second is his home situation. He explains that he has authority over his slaves. He is the head of his home. He has authority.

For a leader to successfully create followship one has to grasp the concept of the differing types of leadership and the differing levels of authority and responsibility.

The first leadership type is the **natural leader**. Generally, in church life, it is my considered opinion that we are not very good at empowering the natural leader. This person, in my experience, is usually not a church leader, but is maybe in business, commerce or is influential in the community. This person sometimes causes the church leader frustrations because they have a natural ability to attract followers. Wherever a natural leader goes, it's as though they have authority. They seem to lead at all times. Before Christ they led the activities in the pub. On Saturdays they lead the activities on the football pitch and on Sundays they can even "lead" what is happening in church life.

Firstly, we need to get these people into church leadership. They are natural leaders. All they need is to be harnessed with biblical principles and the call of God and they could build sensational churches. The problem these natural leaders have is that most church leaders are zonal or positional leaders and the natural leader always has a greater gift of leadership.

The leader must be very intentional and gather these natural leaders and utilise their gifts in helping them to lead the church. Get the natural leaders onside and, if they are being led by the leader, they will lead the followers very effectively.

The second type of leader is the **zonal leader**. The Roman Officer clearly states that in his work situation there is an area, or zone, in which he has authority – not outside that zone, only inside that zone. He was aware that his authority did not lie in the zone that he was talking about to Jesus.

An example of a zonal leader can be best illustrated by someone who is a nurse or First Aider. The church leader holds the authority for what happens in the church on Sunday, but if someone falls over and cuts their head, instantly the church leader looks for the one who has authority in this specific zone i.e. first aid. The church leader is the leader, but is very happy to see the nurse or First Aider operate in their zone of authority. Followers get frustrated when leaders do not, or refuse to, recognise their zone of authority. An intentional leader will discover people's zones. It may be their occupational background or specific training or their qualified background. It may also be a "grace zone" – an area with which God has particularly graced that person for a specific area of ministry or function. The leader needs to facilitate people so that they operate in their zone. Be intentional and watch great followership develop.

The third type of leader is the **positional leader**. This is a person who has authority and responsibility purely because of their position. I regretfully observe that this happens in church life more than any other walk of life. The positional leader may have been given authority and responsibility, but that doesn't make them a leader. They actually don't have the capacity to lead and to take people somewhere, thus they are not able to create followship because there is no leadership to follow. The leader should be on the look out for the positional leader. I'm afraid the reality of it is that the leader needs to remove this type of person from their position, otherwise they will be a bottleneck in the organisation that will strangle followership in that particular area. The kindest thing to do for the positional leader and their followers, who aren't being led, is to intervene in the situation and bring change, thus freeing the followers from the bottleneck. Then place a leader in that position who will stimulate followership because the followers now have leadership to follow.

4.3 | Checks and Balances |
Ps Becky Galloway

Accountability in church life is so important and often not addressed for many reasons — maybe ignorance, a "small church" mindset, or because the senior leader themselves fears the thought of being accountable. But we are building God's Church and using His resources, so it is imperative that we are accountable! Being accountable can massively increase productivity because systems and organisation improve our time management and accountability causes more productivity.

All my life I have tithed into the local house. I believe in this biblical principle, as many Christians do. However, when you are a church leader yourself and employing staff, the responsibility of administering these tithes falls on your head. People in our church faithfully tithe believing and trusting that we (the leaders) will use the money wisely. If I have a staff member who is not functioning well, comes and goes as they please, has no clear job description and has no one who keeps them in check, then I am not being faithful to those who faithfully give their tithes every month. That is a sobering thought and one that must be addressed in church life. All too often I hear of church staff who have no job description!

What?! What well-run business would function like this: paying someone for, well, just a kind of floaty agreement? It wouldn't happen in business and it shouldn't happen in church! We are called to be the head and not the tail, we have brains in our heads, let's sort this out.

Job Descriptions

So rant over, let me now explain how we currently organise our systems and staffing at BCC. Early on, as we started to employ staff, we realised that for their benefit and the church's they needed to know exactly what they were here to do! So all staff members receive an offer letter before they commence work at BCC detailing what their role will include. This is their job description. Sometimes we work with the person we are employing (particularly if it is a ministry post) to design that job description together. I remember doing this with our City Kids Lead. We wanted to reach kids across our city and provide for those within our church. She had some ideas about how this could work. She had more experience of working with kids than we did, but we knew the vision of the church and the big scale picture of what we wanted kids' stuff to look like at BCC, so we worked together and came up with a job description. For administrative based roles the job description isn't negotiable; we know what we need and that is communicated to the employee via their job description.

Contracts

It really bugs me that all over this nation we have people faithfully serving God in their local church and being paid for it, but often being paid well below what they are actually worth. They may have given up a career in order to "serve God", which is great and God will bless them for that. But hang on, we also have a responsibility. All too often those who have spent their life employed by church get to 65 and ... pension? Oh yes, we forgot about that!

"But church budgets were tight ... But they said they didn't mind not having one..." (of course they didn't, because this is generally the heart of people who choose to give up their career to serve God!)

We must think of ourselves as employers and so we need to look after our employees. All our staff members have a generous pension package, because when they get to retirement, I want to know that they are being looked after and honoured for serving God. As a church we shouldn't put the burden of a pension on the state or their family members. It's our responsibility.

So our contracts are legal documents that protect the rights of the church as employers and the staff as employees. Contracts will state holiday entitlement, hours of work, salary and how that salary will increase over time. Contracts will explain the standards that we expect from our employees, as well as misconduct and dismissal rights and procedures.

Salaries

The "hush-hush" subject in church life! When we started employing people we honestly didn't know what to pay them, so we did something quite unwise and just matched the existing salary of wherever they were coming from. In a way this was good, because it set the culture of honouring a worker for his/her worth, but also meant we had a diverse range of salaries. After much research we found there is very little help out there regarding salaries for church employees. Denominations tend to give guidelines for senior pastors, but for administrative staff, ministry staff and executives there are very few suggestions.

So after some hard work by one of the Directors of our Incorporated Charity we came up with pay scales which included brackets for different roles and a ladder system within each bracket. Whilst we were doing this, we happened to be reading in a staff meeting from Bill Hybels' book Axiom. He talks about grading his staff periodically with an A, B, C or D grade. Slowly around the room we began to hear, "Let's do it ... Yeah that would be great ... It'd help us know how we were achieving."

So we introduced performance related pay (at the request of our staff!). Every six months the staff are graded in five areas: their productivity, their passion (heart for the house), how they are carrying the weight of their role, their growth (personally and within their role) and their development and management of team. This grading is marked against their job descriptions and against their aims from the previous six months. The Staff grade themselves and then this is looked at by each person's line manager and presented to myself and James. In order to receive their yearly salary increment they must achieve at least two B grades that year.

If they are consistently achieving C grade, we will look to give the person extra support and training. If D grades become regular we will begin to look at whether repositioning or releasing the person from employment is something that needs to happen.

Many of you reading this book will be familiar with these types of systems in your work place. When I worked for the Council a similar system was in place and was considered perfectly normal. At BCC we now consider it normal and an important part of making sure we are being accountable with the resources God has given us.

Holidays

It is important that our staff operate from a place of rest. Like any employee they need a break from time to time. At BCC we insist that holidays are booked every December for the following year. We have a system in place to ensure that key members of staff or primary leaders aren't all away at the same time so that church can continue to function well throughout the year. Staff may take four Sundays off a year as part of their annual leave. More often than not, they don't want to miss Sundays, but we insist that they do!

When staff go away on holiday we encourage them to leave their mobile phones at home and have a real break.

Reporting

You will get the idea by now that we are pretty hot on keeping our staff in check, but it wouldn't be possible to do all we do as a church without a huge army of volunteers. Many of these volunteers hold positions of huge responsibility and so we need to ensure that we are holding them to account and that they are getting the support that they need.

We run a system of monthly reporting throughout the structure of the organisation. Anyone who holds a position of responsibility completes a report. As a church grows it becomes impossible to touch base with every ministry lead or pastor on a regular basis, so for us as senior pastors this is a great way of catching up on what's going on and keeping things in check.

Our reporting system works alongside our organisational structure and is in fact a key part of our operational structure. On a designated day in the month reports are sent to Stream Directors and Pastors, the reports are compiled and a summary report written and the reports passed onto our five Executives (who basically have the responsibility of running the church for us). In turn the Executives compile and complete a summary report which comes to Primary Leadership level.

This means Primary Leaders need only read summary reports rather than hundreds from across the different functions of the house. There are times we may need to dig deeper and look at a report of a particular ministry, but due to the systems in place this is easy to do.

So what do we expect to find in the reports? We make it really easy for our ministries. There is no need for them to find a vision for their ministry or monthly themes or even a yearly scripture – all this is done from Primary Leadership level and every function within the house should be running within these. So we would expect events to be based around the church's monthly themes and always working within the vision of the house. Within the reports it will be documented how many people have been at events (where appropriate), how much finance has been raised and spent; it will detail aims for the forthcoming month and revisit the following month's aims.

In addition to the monthly reports, everyone who has a position of responsibility within the house, whether it be at Executive level, Director and Pastor or Lead level, will have a monthly meeting with their line manger. This meeting is important for the passing on of vision and information from the level above, as well as the development and encouragement of the person in position.

In conclusion, in order for us to function as effectively as possible it is so important to have checks and balances in place. Without them we will not be functioning to our full capacity and that would not give glory to the most excellent God we serve.

4.4 | Triangular Leadership

The conversation regarding being intentional in leadership so as to produce followship became very revealing once I grasped a real understanding of what I've come to term "Triangular Leadership".

When a leader moves forward, steps up, progresses, advances, goes on a journey, develops or whatever phrase you choose, there is instantly space created between the leader and the follower.

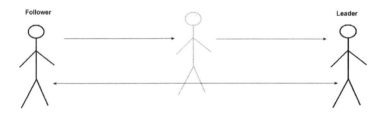

This space that is created by the leader vacating his previous place and stepping up is then made available for the follower to step up into also.

The drastic understanding that there has to be a continuum of parallel development of the leader AND the follower in order for an organisation or church to progress, is evidential. If the leader continues to develop and the follower fails to develop, then the space becomes too great and the leader then fails to be leading and leaves people behind.

Or: if the followers fail to develop and thus fail to keep up, then they leave the leader to walk into the distance and they lose sight of their leadership. Triangular Leadership helped me grasped this for the following reasons.

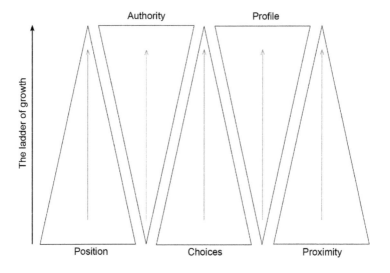

The first triangle "position" helps us begin to understand that in any scenario of leadership there is a progressive nature to the activity. Whether in business, commerce, church, community or even family, as a leader advances in their leadership gift, talent, understanding and acumen, what happens is that their level or positioning increases also. I have not always been the senior pastor of a very fast growing church. I stated earlier that I can remember as a child being on a team of young guys who were responsible for the OHP. I then recall being asked to lead a Kids Church class, leading to involvement on a youth team. Then I got to lead a youth ministry, which grew to thousands, and then I got to lead Youth Alive South Wales, leading to the creation of Selah Youth Network. I then became Executive Pastor of the small church I was a part of and now I find myself leading Breathe City Church. Leadership progresses as the leader progresses.

The higher up the triangle a leader goes, the less the peer level is populated. Up the triangle one goes.

The second triangle, "Authority", shows that even though the peer level is less populated, as a leader advances in their leadership, the greater the authority and the responsibility, as it's a partnership, that rests on a leader's shoulders. It is also hugely significant to point out that a leader has to learn to handle this pressure, weight and privilege. Many a leader wants the position and the authority, but fails to realise that with both comes the responsibility.

Moving to the fifth triangle, "Proximity" shows that as a leader advances in their journey, the less people become a part of the close world around them. This is not that a leader has nothing to do with people, but the reality is, when I was leading a church of 62 people in the congregation, I was able to visit them all in the first month of being here in Stoke-on-Trent. It is now impossible to visit 1,000 people in a month. I do, however, meet with our Pastoral Executive, who has several pastors working for him, and who keeps me informed of certain occurrences that I need to be aware of.

The downside of this is that many young people see mega-church leaders being drafted from one pulpit to another and forget that the leader they are watching has done their time with people first. Many a young leader never grasps the importance of people and simply loving them, and thus will never be able to create followship.

The fourth triangle, "Profile", doesn't merely mean that more people know the leader or that the leader gets more famous. In reality it means that the leader is seen more. The profile of the leader increases. I can be walking in the city centre and not know anyone, but they may well know me. Integrity, right living, character flaws, weaknesses and the like are all up for discussion here. As leaders, very often we are offended by such a comment, but please hear me: in the conversation regarding leaders intentionally developing followship, a leader has to understand that leadership is visual, whether they know they are being watched or not.

How we behave in the restaurant, with our kids, our spouse, what we are reading, the conversations that we have, all have to be very intentional in helping a follower know how to behave. The armour bearer followed Jonathan's example, but the armour bearer didn't know that 600 soldiers and many Hebrews hiding in caves were watching and wanting a model.

Yet the crux of Triangular Leadership is the central triangle: "Choices". It is a leader's choices that determine the advance or the decline of that leader's progress.

Firstly, yes the quality of choices that a leader makes is imperative, but note that the width of the triangle decreases in size as the leader progresses. In other words, the second thing to note is that a leader has fewer choices to make. Or, in regard to followship, chooses to delegate and release far more choices to those following. This does two evidential things:

It clearly ensures that the leader reduces the decision making process to purely focusing on the headline issues and thus delegates to and empowers their followers to thrive in the "space" created. Trust, development, investment and inter-dependence are very much a pre-requisite and cause a leader to be very intentional in creating excellent followship.

It also creates very precious scenarios where a leader entrusts his (or her) weaknesses and blindsides to followship. The reality of this scenario is that, as leaders, we have fewer choices to make due to the great environment that has been created. Armour bearers now say, "No, we'll sort that. You focus on what you're called to do, which is lead. We'll sort the rest."

It also empowers followship to watch a leader's back and protect their leader from making the mistakes that we can all make. The followers are now empowered to follow well, which means as extraordinary armour bearers they are creating a great example and model to those now following them.

Triangular Leadership and this revelation changed not only my leadership and my team's leadership in their armour bearing duties, but created followship across the life of the church.

4.5 | Perpetual Memory

Throughout this section I have attempted to bring practical insights into understanding leadership from a followship perspective. At this point I would like to draw your attention to a differing angle in order to help the leader. Leaders simply lead towards what they see. They live towards their vision and because of the leadership gift on their lives, people follow. Great followship is established if the leader is intentional in helping and empowering their followers to follow.

I re-iterate: *leaders simply lead towards what they see.* Intentionality says that if we can change the way a leader sees, then we begin to change the way a leader leads. This is what I attempt to do here.

The last two verses of psalm 45 created in my thinking a paradigm and strategy regarding how I build church and thus have an impact on the way I lead and the way people follow me. It also, therefore, has an effect on the type of followers that I attract by my leadership.

A side note: leaders have to recognise that they are called to lead. That does not, in any way shape or form, mean that they are called or have the capacity to lead everybody. Leaders lead and followers choose who they are going to follow. Leaders shouldn't get frustrated by this. They should simply lead in a way that followers respond to and respond well!

Here are my observations from Psalm 45:16-17:

"Your sons will become kings like their father.
You will make them rulers over many lands
I will bring honour to your name in every generation
Therefore the nations will praise you for ever and ever."

The first thing is a clear statement that the sons will become kings like their father. In leading this church I ensure, unashamedly, that our whole ethos is geared towards empowering the next generation. Everything we do has a next generation bent. It is done absolutely intentionally and unashamedly. May I be so bold as to challenge the status quo that has helped the Church be primarily made for the middle aged and upwards – that produces a generation that "puts up" with church. The older we get the more mature we should be and we should get to the place where peripheral stuff in church life should take a back seat in our discipleship. For instance, the music and the media, the decor and the publications. SO many church arguments are about superficial stuff that really isn't even in Scripture.

We should be ashamed of ourselves.

Our bent is totally towards making the "now" generation comfortable with the style and presentation of church life. What excites me the most is the volume of older people who transition into the life of this church. They come with several comments such as, "We know it is not designed for our preference, but look at what is happening with our kids and grandkids. We have to be here to endorse it, pray for it and resource it."

That is because of the generational perspective.

Secondly, we get a clear hint of a new expression of authority. *"You will make them rulers over many lands."*

I have intentionally sown this into our Vision Casters and Carriers. There is a new authority coming on the church. We have authority for our cities and communities. We shouldn't criticise what is happening in our locality. It is our responsibility. We have the responsibility because we have the authority. This intentional bent is again manifesting in our activity as a church with so many ministries now functioning and making a difference. What this does for followship is that it provides a reason. People are looking to make a difference. Jesus is looking to make a difference. He told us in the Great Commission to "Go" and we've been asking people to "Come"! We've been praying for a change and God has been telling us to be the change.

God will never do what He is asking His people to do.

The third and final aspect of this chapter that I want to highlight is a real trigger for leaders to become intentional. The final verse states, "I will bring honour to your name in every generation." Other translations use the phrase "perpetual memory".

"Perpetual" means to put forward or to place in front. Memories are thoughts that are crystallised regarding activities we have experienced in the past. What this scripture is directing us towards is that it is possible to have a forward thinking memory.

Let me explain forward thinking memory. This is the ability to do things now that will, in the future, create memories. This is the very essence of intentionality. This is the revelation that we, as the leader, can plant things into the life of the church and city now that will bring benefit and harvest in the future. This requires a leader not merely to experience life and collect memories, but actually sit down and make decisions regarding the memories that, in the future, they would like to possess.

This simply means that a leader doesn't go from pillar to post reacting and responding to every whim that occurs. It doesn't mean that the leader has room to sit and project vision statements in the hope that followers will follow. What it does mean is that if a leader is to develop a forward thinking memory, they must think long and hard about their vision and make decisions about what it will look like in 5, 10, 20 years and even a generation from now. When the leader is very clear in their heart and mind regarding this, they must work tirelessly in plotting out their activity and communication.

Everything from here on in is designed with the future in mind.

Everything that is said must bring fruit in the future.

Every activity that takes place must work towards bringing tangible evidence that the vision is being fulfilled.

The revelation of intentionality means that the leader grasps the revelation that great followship is essential if the vision is to be fulfilled.

A perpetual or a forward thinking memory is a game changer!

.

4.6 | Keys, Money & Mobile Phones

Followship is an amazing phenomenon in which leaders have to have a broader understanding of life, society and where they are going. I want to look at the subject of information and how important intentionality is with regard to the information we give and how it is given.

On Planet Earth right now there are 6.3 billion people and rising. What you may be astounded to know, as was I, is that there are 3.0 billion people who have cellular connectivity – have a mobile phone of some description. Even more fascinating is that a further 1.0 billion will be added to the cellular connected community within the next two years.

Research has been carried out that has produced a global trend which intentional leaders should begin to understand when it comes to information. If I asked you the question, "What do people carry?" Even, "What do you carry?" You may be surprised that there are three definite answers that are always given.

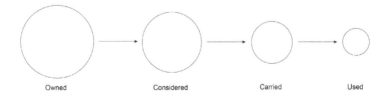

Owned   Considered   Carried   Used

When a person walks out of the door the following process occurs and is illustrated above. Firstly there tends to be an awareness of all that a person "owns". The second movement is that a person "considers" what they should take with them. The third movement is that a person collects and "carries" what they need for their day and the fourth and final movement is what a person actually "uses". A person rarely uses all that they carry; they rarely carry all that they consider; and inevitably a person rarely considers all that they own. We work through filters and narrow things down. The global trend then, is that a person generally leaves the house with three things:

Keys

Money

Mobile phone.

Why is this information important for a leader regarding intentionality and followship?

Walk with me a little further.

The three things mentioned are also usually stored in a place we subconsciously decide upon to ensure we never leave home without them: maybe a kitchen side or a drawer or even the mantel piece. Thinking about it, my place is the 4th stair in our hall way. Yes, it infuriates Becky, but I may talk about that if I ever write a book on marriage!

A person subconsciously "places" that which they don't want to leave the house without, so as to not forget them.

Now, tie the above in with the following.

Since the 1970s, and particularly since the turn of the century, the levels of information available compared to our ability to retain information are incomprehensible.

The reality of the present day situation is that people are absolutely bombarded with too much information – so much so that they don't even hear most of the information that passes them by.

Now you may see where I am going with this.

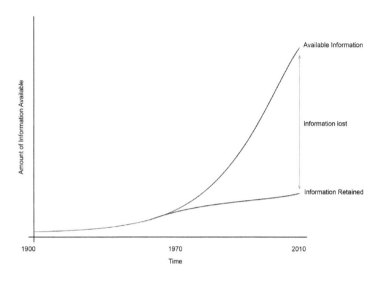

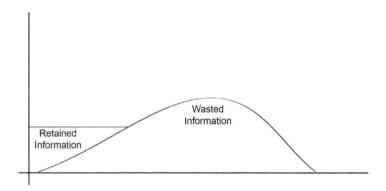

What about the church vision, church diary, the notices, the important message you feel to bring, the large building offering that is coming up or the plans for the summer mission?

Listen.

People are not hearing you.

An intentional leader therefore begins to plot how and what information is going to be given.

Standing at the front on a Sunday and casting vision, sharing information and making requests are no longer viable ways of communication. Leaders must get intentional with communication if followship is to be established.

Here are a few discoveries we have made.

People always leave home with a mobile phone. Texting is huge. Initially group texting worked until we outgrew that phase and BlackBerry Messenger took over. (I wrote about this in section 3.2).

The moments of solitude must be captured. Whether people are on the bus, train, car, their lunch break, even on the toilet, there are moments that can be captured! An e-newsletter, Twitter, free monthly podcasts (of no more than a 20-minute car journey in length) and other bitesize chunks of information can be sent out. These work!

Keep to one simple sound bite that casts the vision for the season you are in. Create a hash tag that identifies the current preaching series. Build the preaching series to help construct the season you are in. Create avatars and visuals everywhere that keep banging that same drum.

Don't highlight everything. What's the one thing, the main thing, that you want people to support this week or this month? Choose your priority and build everything to that one aspect. Give people something as a reminder, let's say creating a wallpaper for their mobile phone that they take with them EVERYWHERE! You get the picture.

Look at your Sunday Schedule. Don't pack ten things in for people to remember, pack one thing in ten times so that it IS remembered. Then repeat it in every aspect of communication throughout that week.

The reality is that if a leader is to be intentional in creating followship, then the leader needs to be communicating in a way that dominates the headlines. People become accustomed to it if the leader is repetitive enough. Now, as soon as a new preaching series occurs, BCCers all start using the same hash tag, avatar and other aspects of communication. It becomes a standard practice for followers to follow.

Habakkuk 2 talks of writing vision on tablets so that "they" (the people) can run with it. This is the old scriptural message again directing activity in the 21st Century. The tablet maybe a PlayBook or an iPad nowadays, but the leader must get it into the hand of the follower so that they can run with it too.

Knowing that people have hectic schedules and that too much information is bombarding them (so much so that they don't even hear most of it), a leader has to manoeuvre the communication of the church to ensure that, in the same subconscious way each person creates a place to pick up their keys, money and mobile phone, they do so with that regular, repetitious sound bite that you need them to hear and respond to.

Once patterns are established, people begin to hear and respond. Once they begin to respond, they begin to follow.

All because the leader was intentional and not random or suggestive in their communication.

4.7 | Stop Looking For Permission | Rhi Davies, Operations Executive

As a House we have been on a journey to get to where we are now and we are continuing on that journey to where we're going. One thing is vital no matter where you are on your journey: you, your team and your church needs to stop looking for permission. You need to rewire your thinking. You need a "make it happen" mindset.

A make it happen mindset changes everything. Obviously, it changes the way you think, but it also changes the way you see, the way you talk, the way you act and the way you live. It changes you and as a result it changes the church. With a make it happen mindset you won't settle for the "what if's", you won't think in "if only's" and you won't accept that "impossible" applies to you. Instead, you will live out that "all things are possible" – it's simply a matter of seeking out the how.

How you develop a make it happen culture starts with you as an individual and then spreads contagiously across your teams. It begins with an unwillingness to settle for what is, a belief that there has to be more, and a recognition that settling for good is the enemy of great.

Who you are

Being a make it happen person requires you to be fully you, because it is only when you're fully you that you can give yourself fully.

Hezekiah tried to obey God in his service of the Temple of God and he tried to obey God's teachings and commands (2 Chronicles 31:21 NCV). He gave himself fully to his work for God, so he had success.

Hezekiah gave ALL his heart and in giving all of it he prospered and so too did an entire nation.

In reality there is a cost to everything in life. Nothing is free and making things happen has a price. Someone is going to have to pay somewhere, so why shouldn't that someone be you? If your answer to that question is, "Well, because…" then are you truly giving all of who you are? Don't hold back. Give everything and then give everything.

"Don't think you have to put on a fund-raising campaign before you start. You don't need a lot of equipment. You are the equipment…" Matthew 10:9-10 (MSG).

We need to live in the realisation that we are all that we need and therefore we are not restricted by material goods or finance. Simply who we are is sufficient to make things happen.

How you view…

How we view things often determines our response. For example: we see something funny and we laugh; we see cooking programmes on TV and the next thing we're in the kitchen knocking together a three course meal (not so much in my case!). It's the same with church. How we view it has a significant impact on our response to it. Do we view it as a house or a hotel? BCC is definitely a house and definitely not a hotel. What do I mean by this? In a hotel you are paying for a service. You can have what you want, when you want, and not have to move a muscle. However, in a house you choose to invest – invest finance, time and energy to make it the best it can possibly be. In a house there are things that need to be done and usually those things are only done by those who live there. It's no different in the House of God. We should be investing everything so that it becomes the best that it possibly can be, because it is a house not a hotel.

A make it happen mindset chooses not to see obstacles, but instead sees opportunities and chooses to say yes to seize them. Then it sorts out the logistics. Never let the logistics determine the opportunities you seize. Have the faith to say "yes" because when God-given opportunities come along we rarely have everything else in place – and that's the thrill of a make it happen mindset.

What you've got

To establish a make it happen mindset you need to be willing to use exactly what you've got. What's in your hand? Don't hold on to it, unwilling to let it go, use it! In reality it doesn't really matter exactly what is in your hand; it matters simply that you use it. I love that in Matthew 25 we see the parable of the talents and then, in the very next chapter, we read the story of the woman with the alabaster jar.

In Matthew 25:26 (MSG) it says,

"The master was furious, 'That's a terrible way to live! It's criminal to live cautiously like that!'"

Then in Matthew 26:9 (MSG) the disciples respond to the pouring out of perfume by saying, "That's criminal."

Unfortunately, at that moment they'd missed the point.

The fact is that it's criminal to live cautiously. It's criminal to NOT use what's in your hand.

The woman with the jar used exactly what was in her hand, regardless of the personal cost, and as a result her deeds are recorded for eternity.

A make it happen mindset uses exactly what's in its hand and uses it to its maximum capacity, always believing that being faithful in the small things will result in more being given.

Rise to the challenges

A make it happen mindset rises to the challenges placed before it, which makes for an absolutely awesome adventure!

Life was never intended to be dull. When we rise to challenges, enthusiasm is demonstrated and that becomes contagious. It spreads through a team like wildfire. It crosses generations and enables the impossible to become possible. Rising to the challenge isn't about success or failure, because even the smallest something is better than the biggest nothing. It's easier to get forgiveness for your attempt than it is to get approval for your inactivity.

Rising to the challenge doesn't even count the cost. It's a willingness to push the boundaries of the possible and exceed the expectations placed before it. Rising to the challenges lets us know we're alive.

So stop looking for permission and make it happen.

4.8 | Dying Church and "5"

The other night I was being a little reflective regarding the awesome journey that we are on here at Breathe City Church and it again dawned on me how privileged we are.

I have a weekly discipline of blogging on activity regarding this privileged adventure but, during the other night's musings I realised that, for me, it hasn't always been this way. I again realised that I have been part of the struggle in church life where it's tough, demoralising and extremely frustrating.

What you are about to read is not meant to be condescending or patronising.

I can write this sincerely because I genuinely know what it is to be in that difficult place. I hope this helps...

Have you ever asked the question regarding why God called out to Adam, in Genesis 3:9, *"Where are you?"*

Like, as if God didn't know?

Well yes, of course God knew ... but did Adam know?

Very often, in my experience, church fails to break through because it fails to recognise where it is.

In my experience, regarding church, the best way to bring something to life is to first recognise that it's dead.

So this may be tough, but if I am intentional in helping you, the reader, to develop in leadership and thus create great followship, then I have to address this.

This is purely based on experience and will hopefully help you to discover some harsh realities that I wish I had been told years ago.

Here are five items of evidence that the church is dying and five ways to combat them:

One: A Lack of External Influence

For me, this was the start of my recognising dying church. When a church or leader becomes an island, they become isolated from what is happening elsewhere in Christendom. What happens is that they begin to set the rules of what is "alive" simply because there are no comparisons to be had. An "alive" church will be bringing in the best speakers and have relationships with churches, people, leaders and organisations who are bigger, more prolific and who add value to the life of the church. A lack of external influence begins to occur when insecurity begins to set in. It is such a small thing, but it's SO big.

COMBAT IT: Simply get alongside people who make you feel insecure! Pastor David Shearman once told me, "Learn to dine with the big boys" and this is so true. Invest in yourself, go to conferences, travel. Invest in your church and get the leading ministries on the planet to come to you! Kill this insecurity before it takes over.

Two: The Demonizing of Growing Churches

It's amazing how I was conditioned to do this. Now, looking back, I see that it was so wrong. What happens is that to justify the lack of "success/growth/achievement" one simply sees others who are having a significant impact as a threat, and so you demonize them. They must, you reason, be doing something wrong, so you begin to utter phrases like, "It's man made ... It's so fake ... It's manipulative ... I know a guy who used to go there and he says..." and so on. I was so guilty of this for many a year in a previous life.

Now I simply recognise it as a sign that the church was dying. Listen: ALL HEALTHY THINGS GROW!

COMBAT IT: Begin to celebrate the success of others. Speak highly of people and the great things that are happening around the nation. All demonising will do is eat you up inside and it definitely won't stop the success of others. In fact, from my experience, they will grow even faster as God begins to do a work in you. You reap what you sow. If you want success then celebrate other people's success.

Three: Loyalty to the Pastor Because of History Not Future

When a church leader uses fear of the unknown, history, or "be planted and you'll prosper" type phraseology, then death is occurring. Jesus said, *"You do not want to leave too, do you?"* (John 6:67). A dying church keeps people because they feel bad about leaving. I was in this situation for a long time. Listen: loyalty to death leads to death ... being planted in unfruitful soil leads to ... well, you get the idea.

COMBAT IT: Have the conversation. Say what needs to be said. Understand that you don't "have to" do anything – you are free to "choose to". Leave. Stay. It's your call, but make the decision because you have made the decision. Choice is linked to life. Deuteronomy 30:19-20 says, *"Now choose life, so that you and your children may live."*

Four: The 2nd Row Struggle

This, for me, is the ultimate sign that a church is dying. When those in the second row are frustrated, when the young people are bored but disguise it with being spiritual, when the associates/youth pastors/2nd tier leaders are trying to bring the change ... then it's over! When followship is attempting to be leadership then we have a crisis. What this shows is that the leaders are *on top* and not *in front*. I say this, aware of potential criticism, but I am more passionate about this than any of my critics realise. I have experienced it and I have scores of 2nd tier leaders from around the nation talking to me on this subject. Change does not come from the 2nd row. For years I would say, "Serve and stick in there," to many a 2nd tier leader, many of whom are now not in church at all because of burnout, frustration, bust ups and the like. This is a sure sign of death.

COMBAT IT: 2nd tier leader – have the honest conversation with your senior. Then commit to serve and lay aside your frustrations ... or leave. The church will never go the way you want it to go ... it's not your responsibility! Your senior pastor is responsible, not you. So either serve his vision diligently or leave. Otherwise division, disharmony and discord will follow. Followship is best at following and leadership is best at leadership. Crossing roles doesn't work. It is that simple.

Five: The "Sheep Stealing" dialogue

The reality is, many a person moves from one church to another. In a healthy environment a church and its leadership will help transition a person to where they feel called or led.

However, a tell-tale sign that a church is dying is when the accusation is levelled that the church down the road or across town is "Sheep Stealing".

In our experience here at Breathe City Church, we have had this said about us many, many times – even though 70% of our growth is "new birth". It is therefore my conclusion that sheep stealing doesn't exist, merely "sheep keeping". Regarding followship, a leader must not enforce that a person follows. That is control and manipulation, birthed out of insecurity or even narcissism.

COMBAT IT: If the inclination is to criticise the growing church down the road or across town using the term "sheep stealing", don't! Begin to become a sending church. When a leader empowers followers to make their own decisions, followship occurs. Don't speak against, give people something to follow. If people are leaving, it's because they are choosing to follow elsewhere. Celebrate this and at the same time start leading in such a positive fashion that followship is revived and death is diminished. Watch the congregation start to thrive when the leader leads!

If any of the above is evident then intentionality says to immediately combat it ... or the church will die.

4.9 | Breaking the Rules and Invisible Ceilings

As I have already stated several times, Jesus said, "I will build my Church." In the story of Mark 2 we see a paralysed man carried to a house where Jesus was. His friends who were carrying him couldn't get him in to meet Jesus, but that didn't stop them. They climbed to the roof and lifted the ceiling.

It is my absolute conviction that Jesus is building His Church and when Jesus is in the house no ceiling or restriction can stop what Jesus wants to happen.

I would conservatively estimate that most people would agree with what I have just written. Paradoxically, it seems that the Church constantly faces ceilings or restrictions and rules that seem impossible to break. Occasionally gravity can be defied, but in the end it always gets its way. It is thought that the Church is always facing the gravity of "impossibility thinking".

Therefore, putting the above two trails of thought together, it is possible to see that there must be things that we allow to get in the way. Intentionality says that if followship is to be fearless in seeing a vision fulfilled, then the leaders need to example that same unrestrained pursuit of the vision.

Also based on the above, I therefore consider that it is not the things that we are not doing that prevent breakthrough in church life, but quite the opposite. I believe that it is the things that we are doing that are restricting us. The balance has to be addressed so that breakthrough thinking becomes the norm. We are clearly told that, *"As a man thinketh, so he is"* (Proverbs 23:7). Therefore in addressing mindsets we also address behaviour.

Address the mindset of Leadership; address the mindset of Followship.

Completely out of context, the story of David in 2 Samuel 11 gives us an insight into what can be stopping leaders (and therefore followers) from breaking through.

We know the story of David and his moral failing with Bathsheba. This tragic story didn't simply happen, it was a gradual process. In regard to protecting leaders from moral failure the following is helpful. Note that I am still angling this at what prevents leaders and followers from fulfilling that which they are called to fulfil.

The first thing is that David was distracted by somebody who was beautiful. I'm going to state the obvious here. Ugly things don't distract. That which is attractive draws the attention of a leader and thus affects followship.

A father figure of mine, Pastor David Shearman, is fond of quoting the Stephen Covey axiom, "the main thing is to keep the main thing, the main thing." There are so many tugs for the church's attention. There is so much to focus upon. However, a breakthrough church is one that keeps absolutely singular in its focus and pursuit. To get derailed because something or someone else gets the attention instead is a tragedy. We have to keep our eyes firmly fixed on Jesus and the vision to which God has called us. The more profile that we receive means the more adulation and criticism will be thrown at us. Our experience says to listen to neither. Keep harnessed. The greater the recognition, the more opportunities there will be. If the opportunity does not fulfil the purpose and vision of the church, however, move on. Allow the church to see this modelled at leadership level and followship will also become as singular in its focus.

David was in sin. He was doing what was wrong and still couldn't see it. It took a friend to challenge him. Things got distorted. Sin affects your focus, absolutely, but so does pressure. The pressure of finance for example. The reality is that maybe for a generation we will have to get used to building church in an economic climate that we have not seen for a generation.

Intentionally we determined to refuse to live restricted by finance. We concluded that we could never have enough money to fulfil the vision and therefore we should never set the vision within the confines of our budgets. This is difficult to do, but the key is to put wise and frugal financial systems and safeguards in place and then run with the vision. We ensure that every ministry and campus seeks to be self-financing and the whole church now operates with a "don't drain the main" philosophy. Never be distracted!

In 2 Samuel chapter 9 we see David mourning his best friend's death. At these times it is so difficult to keep correct practice; everything gets confused. Disappointments in church life can really rock the boat.

Due to several initial disappointments we made an intentional decision never to allow disappointments to affect the life of the house. We became determined to build this into the framework of our activity with a "hit back harder" approach. If anything tough happens in the life of the church, we instantly respond with a "hit back harder" action. These are really elaborate, even audacious actions or events that propel people's focus on to Jesus and a celebration of victory! This removes the melancholic spirit from the church because when something bad happens, we instantly hit back with something GOOD – and we do it bigger!

The final principle here is detachment. We see in 2 Samuel 11:1 that David was not in the place he should have been. He was detached. It says, "When kings normally go off to war..." Well, David wasn't off at war. Make a conscious decision not to get detached. In our leadership we have uttered the same phrase many times over and now this is pushed through the whole pastoral structure: "Maintain your disciplines."

One of the practical examples is the "Sunday night lull". Every church pastor knows that the greatest high is usually followed by the greatest lull. Many pastors report that the times they watch things on TV they know they shouldn't watch, is soon after that preach that was possibly one of their best. We recognise that at the pinnacle of victory there soon follows a low moment when life plateaus out again. At BCC we combat this potential detachment with the aide of BBM and Twitter. We have an extraordinarily vibrant Sunday activity. We start every Sunday morning storming heaven together in prayer. We finish every Sunday on BBM and Twitter passing around the tremendous praise reports from the day. All the pastors and ministry directors, congregational leads, staff, executives and leaders engage in this huge silent communication which excites us all. It lasts for an hour or two as all the reports come through. Monday morning is full of knowing that God did something spectacular yesterday and today our city will see the fruit of more changed lives.

Epilogue | #TheSpiritOfThePURPLECOW

(If you've just turned here from the Preface to discover what "The Spirit of the Purple Cow" means, we were already here and knew you'd do it. That's intentionality! So please go back to the beginning and learn what it is be intentional!)

In conclusion, I want to lead you through the journey of a season we had that encompassed, thus far, the fastest growth spurt our church ever had – literally hundreds of people in a period of maybe two months. I want to walk you through it in conclusion to highlight some examples, strategies and obvious intentionality.

I was preaching the series that you have read about in this book entitled #GoGetTheFANTASTICPeople, where we were mandating the church to reach out into their reservoir of relationships and connect people with the house. It was part of our stimulation and massaging of our evangelistic strategy, inspiring people to build the church.

I'm still to this day absolutely amazed by church leaders who don't model or challenge the congregation to look at their relational reservoir and the huge potential of growth that is readily available. It's like leaders think that church will grow by simply existing. It won't!

Listen: don't be afraid of challenging people to go and release the potential of their relational reservoir.

So I'm preaching this series, #GoGetTheFANTASTICPeople and everything is loaded ready to help beat this drum – blogs, hash tags and Twitter feeds, Facebook campaigns, e-newsletters and the like. We were going to bang this drum, baby, like never before! We were primed. I was so psyched to preach this message and boy, did I preach it! The series became a total game changer in the life of our church and we have never been the same.

However, something happened that ran parallel to this that was not planned but, due to its crash landing into our activity, we decided to totally embrace it and run with it. The reality is that we are still running with it in differing forms (as you are about to realize!). I'd be as bold to say that it has also become a "river bank" in the life of Breathe City Church.

What happened was that as I was preaching part one of three in this series, I talked about (or from) a Seth Godin excerpt that I had seen on TED.com, where Seth began to describe how unusual it would be if, when you were driving down a country road, for there to be scores of people pulled up taking photos and creating a fuss. He talked of pulling over to discover what was going on, only to be horrified that all the fuss was over a cow! Like, who pulls over and makes a fuss of a cow?! We see them every day! They actually become invisible.

However, if one of those cows that we see every day and that effectively has become invisible, was a purple cow, then everyone would pull over.

The story is highlighting the need to be being and doing something different in marketing and communications so that the product (or in our case, the message and the church) can be seen and not become invisible.

I was preaching at Campus: City at the 11.00am City Gathering, where there would have been around 500 people or so in attendance. What happened was so BCC it was unbelievable. I told this story and, in the context of #GoGetTheFANTASTICPeople, I said, "We need to develop the spirit of the PURPLE COW!"

Spontaneously, the whole 11.00am City Gathering erupted into making cow noises! Literally, EVERYONE started moo-ing!

It was hilarious! Even now whilst typing I'm smiling at the memory!

It was absolutely a catalyst, a defining moment, a riverbank and a God-moment.

What had happened was that the moo-ing people in that 11.00am City Gathering (and believe me when I say that the news spread fast to our other congregations) had caught hold of something. THEY BROKE OUT of a pattern of clapping, listening, championing and all the other great descriptive words of our congregational activity.

It was more than that.

They gave themselves permission to BREAK OUT of their way of doing things.

They met with the Spirit of the PURPLE cow.

We quickly developed avatars and moved our communication to embrace #TheSpiritOfThePURPLECow and BCCers have been PURPLE ever since – completely free to re-define what it is to be!

BCCers embrace the freedom to be purple, to be unique, to be different, to go against the standard, the accepted, even the expected!

They are free to go get people; free to live free; to be themselves fully … and my goodness, how the church accelerated in its growth from there!

We have never been the same since. It's amazing what God has done because we were spontaneous and alert enough to capture a mere moment in a preach that has propelled us into a new dimension.

So, how am I concluding this book about ,
#TheSpiritOfThePURPLECow?

The thing that I want to leave with you, the reader, is this:

You don't have to build church, whether as a leader or a follower, in the ways that are expected, accepted or "standardised".

Listen: be intentional in creating followship.

Trigger the moments, develop the momentum, speak intentionally, prepare the ground, don't hope for a 25% return on vision, don't only see the armour bearer and don't settle for how it's always been.

Be intentional.

Think ahead. Think about what is to be done to cultivate the ground. Plant seed where you know it will produce. Use your communication wisely and get a 100%. Watch the 600 soldiers come from under the pomegranate tree. Welcome those who could be described as "Hebrews who have been hiding in the caves" when they start following.

Be intentional.

Yes it is about Leadership.

And yes it is about Followship.

Followship is most definitely a reality and it can be created.

Be INTENTIONAL.